The Catholic Teacher

Also Available from Bloomsbury

The Catholic Teacher

Teaching for Social Justice with Faith, Hope, and Love

James D. Kirylo

BLOOMSBURY ACADEMIC
LONDON • NEW YORK • OXFORD • NEW DELHI • SYDNEY

BLOOMSBURY ACADEMIC
Bloomsbury Publishing Plc
50 Bedford Square, London, WC1B 3DP, UK
1385 Broadway, New York, NY 10018, USA
29 Earlsfort Terrace, Dublin 2, Ireland

BLOOMSBURY, BLOOMSBURY ACADEMIC and the Diana logo
are trademarks of Bloomsbury Publishing Plc

First published in Great Britain 2023

For legal purposes the Acknowledgments on pp. xix–xx constitute
an extension of this copyright page.

Cover design: Grace Ridge
Cover image © meanderingemu / Alamy Stock Photo

Bloomsbury Publishing Plc does not have any control over, or responsibility
for, any third-party websites referred to or in this book. All internet addresses
given in this book were correct at the time of going to press. The author and
publisher regret any inconvenience caused if addresses have changed or sites
have ceased to exist, but can accept no responsibility for any such changes.

A catalogue record for this book is available from the British Library.

A catalog record for this book is available from the Library of Congress.

ISBN: HB: 978-1-3502-4618-8
        PB: 978-1-3502-4617-1
        ePDF: 978-1-3502-4619-5
        eBook: 978-1-3502-4620-1

Typeset by Integra Software Services Pvt. Ltd.
Printed and bound in Great Britain

To find out more about our authors and books visit www.bloomsbury.com
and sign up for our newsletters.

*For all Catholic educators (and all educators of good will) who recognize
teaching as a sacred vocation, as an adventure that touches eternity
and
For Walter John and Maria Christina
This eternal adventure started with you
Thank you*

Contents

Foreword

As a person who has been brought up in a Roman Catholic environment and received his formal initial education in Catholic schools, at first the nuns of St. Joseph of the Apparition (Primary) and later Jesuits (secondary), it gives me great pleasure to provide the opening comments to this book. I write during a week in which my focus has been precisely on what we call the prophetic church. This was because of a good friend in Brazil, Frei João Xerri, who passed away exactly a year ago and whose first death anniversary has just been commemorated. He belonged to the prophetic church.

It is this church that enabled me to develop a revitalized sense of faith, initially through my reading and deriving inspiration from Paulo Freire, about whom James D. Kirylo and I have written profusely, and later, in my case, Don Lorenzo Milani, Fr. Jimmy Tompkins, Dorothy Day, and more recently Frei Betto. By the time I had personally met and started reading Frei Betto (Carlos Alberto Libanio Christo), in 1998, I had been very much attracted to liberation theology, which made me see the Catholic Church itself as a site of struggle just like any other institution that forms part of the power structure in many parts of the world.

The question which Freire posed to many like me regarding on whose side am I when I teach, a question that also concerns the broader, all-encompassing act of living, applies also to that institution that is the Church, whatever the denomination, or any other faith institution for that matter. The struggle for voice is a struggle encountered in many institutions. People such as Cornel West have rightly spoken about the Church of Empire, the Constantinian Church, which had stopped being the Church of the Oppressed as it moved from margin to center for a variety of reasons including, alas, power considerations.

A once persecuted movement, it gradually spread throughout the Empire to reach the stage when Emperor Constantine and his dominant ruling elite had to come to terms with it to keep his sprawling Roman domain intact. From a largely subversive force, partly driven by charismatic authority, it reached the heart of the power structure, infiltrating and changing institutions in the process. It [the Church] became a hegemonic force, supplanting others as the dominant belief system throughout the empire. Like most belief systems that undergo this process, it became institutionalized, its actions routinized and its structures marked, in Max Weber's terms, by not only spiritual but also legal-rational bureaucratic authority. Rationalization occurred. It became an integral part of a Westernized imperial apparatus involved in the quests for further territories across the globe.

Carried in tow, however, are those who would cling to precepts surviving from the original calling, that is, the persecuted movement, the persecuted Church, the Church of the oppressed. While the most materially influential would be inextricably connected with the powerful, there would be those who still see themselves as being on the side of the least positioned socially, the oppressed, in Paulo Freire's words; the wretched of the earth, in Fanon's; and, the "poor Christs" (I poveri Cristi), as Danilo Dolci would call them.

For every conquistador, there would be a Bartolomé de las Casas; for every suppression of Indigenous people, treated as soulless beings and destined to perdition, there would be Jesuits expelled from different parts of the world for being in solidarity with them; for every Dominican involved in the "Holy Inquisition," there are others who engage in dangerous pastoral work striving with "the meek who shall inherit the earth"; for every Don Abbondio, weak and looking askance at travesties of justice, there will be a Fra Cristoforo who looks the powerful straight in the eye, speaking truth to them.

And, in many cases, there are those who give up their most precious possession, life, for struggling on behalf of and with the poor—your Camillo Torres Estrepo fighting with the oppressed and mowed down in Colombia; Óscar Arnulfo Romero challenging his El Salvadorean brethren to lay down their arms to obey a law greater than the temporal, greed-driven one; Ignacio Ellacuría and his fellow

Jesuit brethren and an unfortunate mother and her daughter, at the wrong place at the wrong time. They were all gunned down because the Jesuits preached a politics of hope and a theology of liberation in the face of mass dehumanization. For every pastor engaging in what I call a form of US-driven, evangelical, "soft" imperial cultural politics, in cities and favelas, there is a Frei Betto empowering people to resist, create, and exercise "the right to govern" in the pastoral centers at Santo André, São Bernardo do Campo, and São Caetano in the state of São Paulo.

I was introduced to Frei Betto by my then new friend Frei João Xerri, whose first anniversary of his passing was commemorated on Tuesday May 31, 2022. Known in his native Malta as Fra Gwann (Friar John, a fully ordained priest who attests to his vows of poverty and humility by adopting what should be the Dominican title of Fra or Frei), João embodied the revolutionary spirit of Christianity as explained above. He risked life and limb in Brazil in championing the cause of landless peasants. He visited and intervened in conflict zones. He often did this in connection with the Pastoral Land Commission.

Frei João was close to the MST (Movimento Trabalhadores Rurais Sem Terra), the landless peasant movement, whom I once saw in Rome as he placed a rose on Antonio Gramsci's grave, on the seventieth anniversary of his death. Gramsci is buried at the *acattolico* cemetery (British American cemetery, with Keats, Shelley, and other luminaries) not far from the Church and Priory of Santa Sabina, on the Aventine hill, where Frei João served for a while. I would later see him, in our home city, Valletta, Malta, sporting an MST cap during a demonstration against the Israeli bombing of Gaza. His presence and MST paraphernalia reflected the bonding that has existed between two landless people, the dispossessed camponesas/os of Brazil and the equally disenfranchised Palestinians, both victims of "settler colonialism."

Frei João embodied a decolonizing version of Catholicism, which entails the struggle against social injustice in this world where faith is lived as a "liberating praxis" and where forms of social injustice are regarded, by Gustavo Gutiérrez, as "sinful." His was a belief, though reinforced by contemporary Gospel resonances, in a faith that connected with the quotidian struggles of common folk. What he embodied was very much that sense of "street church," a grassroots church, and a theology which is simple without being simplistic—a "church from below," if you will. Though not perfect, as he, like Pope Francis, openly admits, João embraced the challenge posed by an interpretation of Christianity that necessitates one's being on the side of the socially least positioned. It is the challenge posed to the Catholic educator, to all educators for that matter, as outlined by James D. Kirylo in this book. Once again, faith is here conceived as a liberating praxis.

Peter Mayo
UNESCO Chair in Global Adult Education
University of Malta

Preface

The Autobiographical Lens Channeling This Text

I delight to do your will, my God; your law is in my inner being!

Ps. 40:9

I am Roman Catholic and am proud to have been born into this faith tradition. My parents were the consummate churchgoing people who prioritized raising my seven siblings and me to know the Catholic faith. Every night before bed, we all gathered as a family to pray the rosary. Going to mass on Sunday was not a choice, including the wearing of "Sunday clothes" to church. Catechism was a must, and being an altar boy was part of the plan. Although in my youth I mostly attended school on a US military installation in the Tuscany region of Italy, I also attended a private Catholic boarding school in Rome for a few years.[1]

Growing up, we regularly had priests over our house for meals and even for vacations, as we lived near the Mediterranean Sea. I was baptized within months of my birth, a traditional Catholic thing to do. My first confession (Sacrament of Reconciliation), First Communion (Sacrament of the Eucharist), and Confirmation (Sacrament of Confirmation) took place at the Vatican, with the latter two at the principal altar in St. Peter's—a great honor, to be sure. And on another occasion, meeting Pope Paul VI was a grand, memorable event. Markedly as one who contributed to the social and ethical teachings of the Church, little did I know that Paul VI would be canonized a Saint by Pope Francis in 2018.

During my collegiate years in Utah, I was particularly drawn to stays at a Trappist monastery, a setting overlooked by the Wasatch Mountain Range, where I was showered with contemplative refreshment (see Chapter 15). The Trappists (Order of Cistercians) are descendants of the Benedictines who were founded by St. Benedict (480–547 CE) of

Nursia (central Italy). Known as the "father" of Western monasticism, Benedict famously wrote "The Rule of Benedict," which the Benedictine Sister, Joan Chittister, characterizes as wisdom literature on how to live the spiritual life, a monastic way of being, and a contemplative way of doing.[2]

As a young adult, I not only was involved with the Catholic charismatic renewal, playing guitar at church functions, retreats, conferences and pilgrimages to Israel, Greece, Turkey, France, and Italy but I also engaged with nondenominational Christian groups, highlighted by a "born-again" conversion experience, deeply illuminating the sustaining place of prayer and the biblical text in my personal and professional life. One could say I had a *metanoia* experience, a term derived from the Greek *metanoiein*, which suggests a conversion or change of mind in which— as expressed in the epigraph—delighting in doing God's will becomes the accent that guides movement. And while the power of a *metanoia* experience can be a one-time event, the journey of that experience is an unfolding lifelong process necessarily grounded in intentionality.

After my first two years of teaching at a K–6 public school setting in a small coal-mining town in southwest Utah, I joined the Missionary Servants of the Most Blessed Trinity in rural Alabama as a lay volunteer, living in community with priests, brothers, and other volunteers. I taught at a small Catholic school and coached basketball, working with students who came from underserved communities. When that remarkable experience came to an end, I relocated to New Orleans, looking toward the possibility to becoming a priest with a move into what was then called the Pope John XXIII House of Discernment, a facility on the grounds of Notre Dame Seminary, where I participated in the daily liturgy and other activities. A thoughtful, prayerful time, to be sure, but God had other plans.

I taught K–12 education for eighteen years, fifteen of which were in a variety of public-school settings and three at a couple of different Catholic school dioceses. Throughout my teaching experience—spanning urban, suburban, and rural settings in three different states—one of Jesus's statements in particular influenced my thinking: "Whatever you did for one of the these least brothers of Mine, you did for Me."[3] Teaching with the goal of radiating faith, hope, love, compassion, and understanding provides a warm conduit to meaningful connect with students and their families. This same mindset grounded me as I moved into my work as a university professor.

It was only after a couple of years working at the University of Alabama at Birmingham (UAB) that I sensed a distinct divine urge to respond to Jesus's exhortation to "[sell] all I had and follow him," a path that took me to teach and work in Paraguay.[4] A land-locked country referred to as the heart of Latin America, Paraguay has a rich history, particularly with the seventeenth- and-eighteenth-century Jesuit missions in their work with the Guaraní, a depiction that was powerfully spotlighted in the 1986 motion picture, *The Mission*. In addition to the beautiful soundtrack by the late Ennio Morricone (1928–2020), the film's exquisite scenery depicted the majestic Iguazú Falls, which borders Paraguay, Brazil, and Argentina.

A Liberation Theology Prism

When my sixteen-month stay in Latin America came to an end, I was back on North American soil, leaning into developing the idea of reflective educational practice in the light of faith, with a continued attentiveness "for the least of these." Liberation theology provided a particular lens that informed my thinking. In brief, theology is the formal discipline to explain God, a process of "faith seeking understanding" as classically conveyed by St. Anselm (1033/34-1109);[5] thus, liberation theology is an explanation of God through the eyes of the poor and oppressed.

Known as the "father" of liberation theology and hailing from Peru, Fr. Gustavo Gutiérrez "realized from the beginning that a theology that does not come out of an authentic encounter with the Lord can never be fruitful."[6] In that light, therefore, as one examines the spirituality, life, and work of Archbishop Óscar Romero (1917–80), it is only natural to conclude that the liberation theology he lived was grounded in a deep encounter with Jesus Christ.

Moved by Romero's courageous commitment to live the Gospel message, I was compelled to spend some days in El Salvador, a country riddled with a violent history in which those living in extreme poverty were subjected to death squads, military repression, and torture for speaking out because of an unjust, inequitable, and unequal political and social system. Enter Archbishop Óscar Romero, who became a powerful voice for the voiceless and took what the Franciscan Richard Rohr calls the naked position of the Gospel—that is, not pleasing the political left or the political right.[7]

Rather, the central focus of his bishopric was one to transparently illuminate reality in such a way as "to bring glad tidings to the poor … to proclaim liberty to captives … to let oppressed go free."[8] Assassinated for bravely asserting his voice, Romero left an inspirational legacy that has risen in the Salvadoran people—indeed, a universal inspiration for social justice workers the world over.[9] It is no surprise that Pope Francis declared Romero a martyr in 2015, which led to his beatification in that same year and to canonization as a saint in 2018.

Who Do You Say That I Am?

One day in Caesarea Philippi, located in northern Israel, Jesus asked his disciples, "Who do people say that I am?" They said in reply, "John the Baptist, others Elijah, still others one of the prophets." And he asked them, "But who do you say that I am?"[10] For the first question, it appears Jesus is asking the question to simply see what the "word on the street is," and to hear it from the perspective of his disciples. It is the latter question, however, that is most interesting and one that must be underscored, unlike the first question, which requires only a simple response.

One would think that after being with Jesus for a while the disciples would have had a pretty good idea who this Jesus was, obviating the need for the question in the first place. After all, these individuals walked with him, dined with him, and followed him. If anyone should have known who Jesus really was, it would be his closest followers.

Nevertheless, Jesus presses with the question, "Who do you say that I am?" The question is personal. It suggests taking a position. And it is the same question that he asks his followers to this day. Peter responded by declaring, "You are the Messiah" (the Christ, the chosen one). In his commentary on that very question, Gustavo Gutiérrez makes the following point:

> To profess "Jesus," to acknowledge "Jesus the Christ," is to express a conviction. It is not simply putting a name and a title together; it is an authentic confession of faith. It is the assertion of an identity: the Jesus of history, the son of Mary, the carpenter of Nazareth, the preacher of Galilee, the crucified, *is* the Only Begotten of God, the Christ, the Son of God … To the question "Who do you say that I am?" we cannot give a merely theoretical or theological answer. What answers it, in the final analysis, is our life, our personal history, our manner of living the gospel.[11]

As I thusly consider my life, my personal history, and the manner in which I live the Gospel message, I understand myself as one who is in a continuous process of becoming, realizing my identity in Jesus, the Christ. In other words, the more I look to know who Jesus is, the more I come to know who I am. St. Teresa of Ávila (1515–82) puts it this way: "As I see it, we shall never succeed in knowing ourselves unless we seek to know God."[12] Our seeking to know God is sustained in relationship with him, through prayer, the reading of Scripture (and other related readings), and in communion with others who are like-minded, coupled with those who may challenge our thinking.

And in knowing God, we come to understand the dialectical interweaving of contemplative living and being immersed in the world. Being immersed in the world not only beckons me to consider my work as an educator but also calls me to be aware of the broader scope of the religious, social, and political landscape, which necessarily suggests position-taking involvement.

In that light, while this book lightly touches on themes related to instructional approaches, curriculum, and other conventional schooling matters, it will also be broad in scope, exploring "out-of-the-classroom" topics, yet naturally intersecting with—and perhaps even challenging—our epistemological and ontological ways of interacting with the world. Indeed, to be a teacher is to be involved both inside and outside of the classroom. To be a Catholic teacher is to filter that involvement through a lens shaped by a lived faith.

Acknowledgments

For many years, I thought about writing this book, and this was the evident moment whose time has come. I want to thank Mark Richardson at Bloomsbury, who has been always open to my various project proposals. I don't take that for granted. Also, from Bloomsbury, thank you, Anna Elliss, as you have been good to work with, guiding me through the production process. Finally I would like to thank Balaji Kasirajan, Senior Project Manager, who brought this work to final publication.

In addition to the helpful suggestions I received from blind reviews, I would also like to gratefully acknowledge Profs. David Armand, Jerry Aldridge, Peter McLaren, and Kathy Fite for reading drafts of the work and offering helpful comments and suggestions. I am grateful for Rabbi Meir Muller, who was especially helpful with his review on the sacredness of life chapter. I am appreciative of Father Peter Sousa, pastor of Our Lady of the Hills Catholic Church in Columbia, SC, for his helpful remarks on this work.

Thank you, Prof. Carolina Fuentes González, Prof. Petar Jandrić, Sr. Marie Pappas, and Fr. Richard Rohr for your respective endorsements. Truly, an honor. Fr. Richard in particular has been extremely influential on my spiritual formation for the last thirty years or so. As I was writing this book, my two sons and I spent a beautiful moment with Fr. Richard at the Center for Action and Contemplation in Albuquerque, New Mexico, a center he founded nearly forty years ago.

Also influential on my faith journey have been, among others, Dorothy Day (1897–1980), Mother Teresa (1910–1997), Archbishop Óscar Romero (1917–1980), Paulo Freire (1921–1997), Pope John Paul II (1920-2005), Martin Luther King, Jr. (1929–1968), Fr. Henri Nouwen (1932–1996), Francis of Assisi (1181/82–1226), Thérèse of Lisieux (1873–1897), Fr. Emile Lafranz (1983–1995), Lisa Wallace, Fr. Gustavo Gutiérrez and Bishop Robert Muench.

Thank you, Prof. Peter Mayo for your insightful Foreword, linking my work to the activism of the Italian priest Fr. Lorenzo Milani (1923–67), to the Brazilian educator and philosopher Paulo Freire, and the thinking of liberation theology. Indeed, teaching for social justice with faith, hope, and love demands the dialectical interweaving of faith and action.

Thank you Nydia María Agudelo Castro for your support on this project. Means much. Thank you, Fr. Richard Jacobs for taking the time to read the manuscript, which led you to make the connection between Prof. Emerita Merylann "Mimi" J. Schuttloffel and me. Thank you, Prof. Schuttloffel, for your incisive Afterword, providing a beautiful bow on what I looked to convey in the totality of this text. Finally, I am deeply grateful for my two sons, Antonio and Alexander. May you continue the journey of faith, wherever it may lead.

Introduction

There is a certain assumption guiding the direction of this book; though it may be obvious, it merits affirmation: spirituality should be considered not as bifurcated, something separate from our private lives relative to our public lives, but rather as a way of seeing life as a whole.[1] To state it differently, spiritual development, as an ongoing dynamic of learning and growing, is not a process compartmentalized from the world and what it means to be a human being; as members of the human family, spirituality is something we innately possess, and something in which we have a natural impulse to live.[2] In the end, living the spiritual dimension of our lives leads us to live deeper in the world.[3]

Therefore, while this book is written for "the Catholic teacher" as its primary audience, whether one works in a public school or religious affiliated setting, it is not meant to be exclusionary but rather ecumenical, interfaith, and interreligious in tone. In that way, perhaps the text will be appealing to Catholics and non-Catholics alike; really, it is meant for all those of goodwill. And while I am not a trained theologian nor a member of the clergy and not an official voice speaking for the Catholic Church, I am nevertheless a person of faith, an educator, a curious inquirer, and simply one spoke in the proverbial wheel looking to foster a more just, right, and loving world.

In the writing of this text, I have attempted to walk a thin line, to avoid moralizing yet to advocate a certain point of view within a process that prompts critical thinking and just action as we each grapple with the mysteries, questions, and dilemmas of our internal and external worlds. Of course, I recognize that over its long history, the Church has had its share of corruption and more-than-disturbing activities, flaws, and shortcomings, as any institution does when the human condition figures into the equation. The purpose here is not to focus on those flaws and even grave sins but rather to leave that to the insightful and needed critical work of many others.

Regarding a particular linguistic approach where I use a plural pronoun when referring to a singular noun (e.g., every Catholic teacher is to live their vocation), I take my cue from Thomas H. Groome, who, with the approval of the US National Council of Teachers of English (NCTE), makes the point that this grammatical pattern returns to Elizabethan English.[4] By design I have attempted to keep this text as succinct as possible, but I do include a fair amount of endnotes that I encourage one to read, adding to the fullness of the text. Moreover, the tone of this book is naturally spiritual yet scholarly, as well as approachable, relevant, and practical. Finally, while this book is not designed to be formulaic or prescriptive, it does offer a kind of road map on how the Catholic teacher can firmly ground a mindset, a way of being, and a way of doing in the endeavor to teaching for social justice with faith, hope, and love.[5]

Structure of the Book and Overview of Chapters

This text is divided into four distinct sections, with each section separate in and of themselves, but importantly relevant in contextually framing the book as a whole. Section I, "Know Your Ecclesial Foundation: Engaging with other Faith Traditions, Appreciating the Church's Inclusive Umbrella, and Recognizing Teaching as a Vocation," is comprised of Chapters 1–4. Chapter 1, "The Emergence and Meaning of 'Catholic' in the Catholic Church," provides the historical context of the term "catholic" and its natural relationship to the Catholic Church, which naturally segues into Chapter 2, "That They All May Be One: Ecumenical, Interfaith, and Interreligious Dialogue," which underscores Jesus's exhortation that we come together as one, a mission that looks to be cultivated through ecumenical, interfaith, and interreligious dialogue. Chapter 3, "An Inclusive Umbrella That Is the Church," highlights how the Catholic Church works to be inclusive in its work with a variety of peoples from around the world. It is within the context of these first three chapters that Chapter 4, "Teaching as a Vocation," is situated. To be a Catholic teacher is to respond to a Divine call, which means not only appreciating what it means to be historically and spiritually Catholic but also realizing the responsibility to lovingly engage with diverse peoples from a variety of faith traditions and other ways of being and to be inspired from examples of so many who know what it means to foster the inclusive umbrella that is the Catholic Church.

Section II, "Know What Informs You: Personalism, Social Teachings of the Church, Liberation Theology, and a Critical Pedagogy in the Light of Faith," includes Chapters 5–9.[6]

Chapter 5, "Looking through a Personalist Lens," discusses the meaning of a personalist philosophy with its link to humanism, underscoring the implications for the Catholic teacher. This personalist lens aids in more meaningfully framing and understanding the social teachings of the Church, the theme for Chapter 6, "An Overview of the Social Teachings of the Church." Providing a historical overview of the church's social teachings gives the Catholic teacher an important context for realizing the connection between these teachings and liberation theology, which is the subject of Chapter 7, "An Organic Link to Liberation Theology." A critical explanation with respect to that link is naturally followed by Chapter 8, "Enabling the Praxis of Liberation Theology." With an understanding of the meaning and intent of personalist thought, the relevance of the church's social teachings, and the organic link to liberation theology, this section culminates in Chapter 9, "A Critical Pedagogy in the Light of Faith."

As expressed in the preface, the work of the Catholic teacher is a vocation both in and out of the classroom. Obviously, one does not stop being Catholic upon leaving the school building; a faith lens necessarily continues to be the filter that informs one's personal, social, and political lives. In that light, therefore, Section III, "Know Your

Positionality: Confronting a Pandemic, Gun Control, Right to Life, and Climate Change," is comprised of Chapters 10–14. Chapter 10, "The Courage to Take a Position," introduces the idea of positionality, articulating the idea that there is a difference between positionality and opinion, which is particularly imperative to recognize when it comes to taking positions on highly charged issues. Chapter 11, "Covid-19 and a Peculiar Toxic Discourse," broadly chronicles the pandemic crises and, in particular, questions those who have sought to undermine the medical and scientific community rather than engaging in thoughtful, civil discourse that works to build the community good toward healing and wholeness.

Chapter 12, "God, Guns, and Country," reflects on the obviously problematic nature of the US gun culture, with a highlight on what the United States Conference of Catholic Bishops (USCCB) and other groups suggest to stem the tide of this uniquely US phenomenon.[7] Chapter 13, "Preserving the Sacredness of Life," presents a historical overview of how the Church came to its position regarding when life begins and what building a culture of life, as Pope John Paul II put it, entails. Chapter 14, "Climate Change and Ecological Conversion," discusses the very real impact of climate change on us, realizing that taking care of the planet falls under the social teachings of the Church, as Pope Francis has emphasized.

Section IV, "Know the Spirituality That Enlightens You," includes only Chapter 15, "Grounded in a Contemplative Way of Being." This chapter emphasizes that a contemplative way of being—one that realizes the place of prayer, obedience, and a dependence on the Word of God— is the well from which the vocation of the Catholic teacher must spring.

A Word about the Book Cover

When I was going about the process of seeking an appropriate cover for this book, I wanted to include something that would be symbolically catching. It didn't take me long to find one that completely caught my eye, an image that expresses a Naïve art form from La Palma, El Salvador. Naïve art is classically represented with its simplicity, non-conventional approach, often depicting cultural contexts, customs, and traditions. And it was the Salvadoran Fernando Llort (1949–2018), a world-famous artist and deeply devout Catholic, who made La Palma, El Salvador, an artistic destination, his home, where he brilliantly filtered his art through a Mayan perspective and the Naïve tradition.[8]

That the illustration on the book cover is a representation from La Palma, El Salvador, therefore, is symbolically meaningful, for—as earlier discussed—El Salvador is where St. Óscar Romero emerged as one of the greatest contemporary saints of our time. Moreover, the image with the bird tending to the flower expresses a certain symbiotic, harmonized relationship, indeed, as in the natural world; each beautifully feeds off the other. In the same way, like a dove metaphorically descending from the heavens to greet humanity, the Holy Spirit desires to nourish and energize each of us through a relationship that is graced with faith, hope, and love; in turn, God is filled with delight with our free-will response to the Holy Spirit's presence, enabling a life of meaning and purpose, paving a very real path toward a more loving, kind, and just world.

Section I

Know Your Ecclesial Foundation: Engaging with Other Faith Traditions, Appreciating the Church's Inclusive Umbrella, and Recognizing Teaching as a Vocation

The Emergence and Meaning of "Catholic" in the Catholic Church

Just as where Jesus Christ is, there is the Catholic Church
Ignatius of Antioch, *c.* 107 CE

After the crucifixion and resurrection of Jesus, the Gospel story tells us he ascended to heaven. As his followers were witnessing the ascension, Luke tells us, "They did him homage and then returned to Jerusalem with great joy."[1] They were indeed given instructions to gather in Jerusalem and the promise that within several days there would be the coming of a paraclete (helper, advocate) or what Christians more commonly refer to as the Holy Spirit. In what amounts to as an extension to his Gospel narrative, Luke continues with his description of biblical history in the Acts of the Apostles, reporting that Jesus's immediate disciples, Mary, and other followers were gathered when "suddenly there came from the sky a noise like a strong driving wind, and it filled the entire house in which they were. Then there appeared to them tongues as of fire, which parted and came to rest on each one of them."[2]

Christianity recognizes the coming of the Holy Spirit as Pentecost, whereby believers were deeply touched so much so that they spoke in different languages and understood one another.[3] This phenomenon left many in great astonishment and others wondering if they were intoxicated from drinking too much wine. A promise of Pentecost was that believers would receive power to witness the faith; Peter boldly spoke that day, touching the hearts of some 3,000 people, who were baptized and came to believe in Jesus Christ.[4]

Pentecost is recognized as the birth date of the Christian Church. Peter, commissioned by Jesus to "tend and feed" his sheep, took an immediate leading role that first day, and the Catholic Church later came to recognize him as the first pope.[5] Subsequent to Pentecost, church communities were founded, and it was later in Antioch (Antakya) (capital of ancient Syria, now in present-day Turkey) in the first century (*c.* 60–90 CE) when for the first time the term *Christiani* (Christian) was used to describe the followers of Jesus.[6]

Later, in the second century, a bishop of Antioch named Ignatius (*c.* 50– between 98 and 117), who followed the bishopric of St. Peter at Antioch, recorded for the first time the word *katholikē* or "catholic" (see epigraph) to identify the followers of Jesus in the collective (or as "the whole") as the Catholic Church.[7] While not much is known about St. Ignatius of Antioch, he wrote seven influential letters to churches on his long journey to Rome, escorted by Roman soldiers who were transporting him to a den of wild beasts as his execution (tradition places this event in the Colosseum) for not renouncing his faith in Jesus Christ.[8]

From Jesus's time to the present day, the Catholic Church has always had an important connection with Rome. Indeed, Saul of Tarsus, who experienced a profound conversion experience on the road to Damascus and is now recognized as St. Paul, was officially a Roman citizen.[9] St. Paul is the credited author for thirteen of the twenty-seven books in the New Testament, including his letter to the church community in Rome, which is "the longest and most systematic unfolding of the apostle's thought."[10] Tradition places St. Paul's death by beheading in Rome sometime between 62 and 64 CE under the reign of Nero, with his tomb located in the Basilica of St. Paul's Outside the Walls Church in Rome. Also, at the hands of Nero, sometime between 64 and 67 CE, St. Peter was crucified and tradition has it that he was executed upside down, and his tomb sits in St. Peter's in Rome, directly a level below the main altar where the Pope celebrates Mass.

While the Catholic Church has historically been linked to Rome, a major geographic move and brewing theological differences within the Church effectively connected the adjective "Roman" to the Catholic

Church. That is, because of Constantine's move of the Roman Empire to Byzantium in 330, because of the great Church schism of 1054 (splitting the eastern church from the west), and because of the Protestant Reformation between the fifteenth and sixteenth century, the intact Catholic Church left standing has been often referred to as the "Roman" Catholic Church (for an overview of these events, see Appendix A). Yet, the official title of the Church simply remains, "The Catholic Church," which is comprised of nearly 1.3 billion people.[11]

The Yeast That Is the Catholic Church

The etymology of the word "catholic" comes from the French *catholique*, from the Latin *catholicus* (universal, general), from the Greek *katholikos*, combining two terms, *kata* (concerning) and *holos* (or whole). The concept of "church" comes from the Greek *ekklēsia* (Latin, *ecclesia*), a term used by the early Greek-speaking Jews, and later on used by the early Christians. The word suggests assembly, originating from the Greek political concept in which the citizens of the *polis* gathered together as a decision-making body. To put it another way, *ekklēsia* (*ecclesia*) is comprised of those who have been "called out" or summoned to gather or assemble for a particular purpose. Thus, the concept of "catholic" has historically been synonymous with the term "Christian" regarding those who have responded to the "call out" with a belief in Jesus Christ, all of whom are gathered (or assembled) as one distinct universal body of people, separate from others.[12]

In an insightful piece titled "Yeast," Walter Ong (1912–2003), the late Jesuit scholar and teacher of English literature and philosophy, notes, as indicated above, that the term "catholic" has been particularly associated with the Latin derivative to mean universal, but then suggests that "equation is not quite exact."[13] In a passage worth citing at length, Ong further expounds:

> If "universal" is the adequate meaning of "catholic," why did the Latin church, which in its vernacular language had the word *universalis*, not

use this word but rather borrowed from Greek the term *katholikos* instead, speaking of the "one, holy, catholic and apostolic church" (to put it into English) instead of the "one, holy, universal and apostolic Church"? The etymological history of *universalis* is not in every detail clear, but it certainly involves the concepts of *unum*, "one," and *vertere*, "turn." It suggests using a compass to make a circle around a central point. It is an inclusive concept in the sense that the circle includes everything within it. But by the same token it also excludes everything outside it. *Universalis* contains a subtle note of negativity. *Katholikos* does not. It is more unequivocally positive. It means simply "through-the-whole" or "throughout-the-whole"—*kata* or *kath*, through or throughout; *holos*, whole, from the same Indo-European root as our English "whole."[14]

Ong continues to explain that *Katholikos* was perhaps used because of its resonance with the passage in Mt. 13:33 (and Lk. 13:21) when Jesus spoke the parable "The kingdom of heaven is like yeast that a woman took and mixed with three measures of wheat flour until the whole batch was leavened."

As a plant that is a fungus, yeast has no defined limits to its borders as it grows. Thus, as an active agent added to dough, yeast allows for expansion, for growth. The image that Jesus painted for his early followers was not lost on them, as they understood that the church, the people of God, possess great possibilities for growth, without borders, without an inclusivity that is contained within itself, separate from others; rather, the kingdom unfolds "through-the-whole" or "throughout-the-whole." In this sense, therefore, the Church is not a "universal" entity, though "certainly 'catholic' in the sense that it has always been in one place or another growing, spreading into new dough, in accord with the parable of the yeast."[15]

Indeed, the yeast that is the Catholic Church is a big umbrella that engages with other cultures, and the yeast from other cultures has graced the Church to growth.[16] For example, in a spirit of ecumenical thought, the Church has drawn from Greek, Jewish, and Eastern philosophies and spiritualties to inform theological perspectives and a variety of ways to express a Catholicity spirituality. In the final analysis, therefore, a certain pluralism is necessary in order for the Catholic Church "to engage the faith in God's real world,"[17] an engagement that has been significantly cultivated through an ecumenical exchange that values interfaith and interreligious dialogue.

That They All May Be One: Ecumenical, Interfaith, and Interreligious Dialogue

We are a multicultural and multi-religious society. Interfaith dialogue provides the glue that nourishes and keeps our society together. As we navigate our diversity, we must learn not to drown or suffocate each other, but instead to swim alongside each other.

Ruhul Amin, 2019

Hours before his arrest, scourging, crucifixion, and death of Jesus, he was immersed in deep prayer with the Father, knowing his hour had come. His prayer centered on how, through his ministry, he engaged the people to come to know him, to know the truth, and to share in the joy and love of knowing God. He also prayed for those witnesses who believed in his word, and for those thereafter who likewise came to believe, exhorting "that they may all be one."[1]

While the exhortation of Jesus is clear, the Church from the beginning has struggled to find unity, to be one.[2] This struggle, however, has not been without a faithful, albeit rocky, effort to find common ground within the Church, to build toward the ideal of a unified whole. For example, consider the growing tensions within the early church, which dealt with questions surrounding the humanity of Jesus, his divinity, and his relationship to God, the Father. Indeed, the first four ecumenical councils (Nicaea, 325 CE, Constantinople, 381, Ephesus, 431, and Chalcedon, 451) collectively looked to bring the Church (Roman Catholicism and Eastern Orthodoxy) into a unified whole through the creation of the Nicene Creed, coming to the common understanding that while Jesus possesses two natures (true God, and true man), he is the only begotten Son of God.[3]

Moreover, despite the Great Schism of 1054, which created a split between the Eastern and Western Church, particularly underscored with the Western Church including the *Filioque* clause into the Nicene Creed, the simultaneous excommunication of Patriarch Cerularius by Pope Leo IX, and the Patriarch's excommunication of the Pope, the two sides nevertheless have worked to reconcile differences (see Appendix A).

Next to the 1054 Great Schism, the sixteenth-century Protestant Reformation dramatically splintered the Church even more. The early murmurings of the reforming movement were to renew the Church from within to maintain its Catholicity, but theological, ecclesiological, and even political differences between the institutional church and the protest movement were too much to overcome. Despite the historic split between the Protestants (as they were called) and the Catholic Church, multiple attempts were made to find unification between the two groups, to no avail. And within the Protestant Reformation, largely due to theological differences, further splits occurred with the formation of separate denominations. Although unification efforts were made throughout the seventeenth and eighteenth centuries, those were also largely unsuccessful.[4]

Emergence of the Modern-Day Ecumenical Movement

However, with the expansion of missionary efforts through Europe, Asia, South America, North America, and Africa in the early part of the nineteenth century and the detrimental effects of a divided church within those efforts, Protestants in particular sought more unity through the interdenominational realm. Bibles were translated in the vernacular of respective countries and widely distributed. The creation of the Young Men's Christian Association (YMCA) in 1844 and the Young Women's Christian Association (YWCA) in 1855 had international appeal, and along with the formation of the Evangelical Alliance in 1846, a path was cleared for a more unified Protestant church. This path was cultivated even more through a global movement of Christian students with the formation of the World Christian Federation in 1895, opening wide the door for the modern-day ecumenical movement.[5]

The 1910 World Missionary Conference at Edinburgh and later in 1921 with the emergence of the International Missionary Council (IMC), which were followed by other conferences and assemblies, set the stage for prioritizing ecumenism well into the twentieth century and beyond. Looking to find common ground regarding doctrinal differences, examining international relationships and economic, industrial, and social challenges in the light of faith, as well as building consensus among Catholics, Protestants, and Orthodox was the framework that captured the collective focus of ecumenical thought. This focus led to the establishment of the World Council of Churches (WCC) in 1948.[6]

Spread out through more than 110 countries and territories, the WCC is comprised of a worldwide community of 349 churches from a diverse group of Christian churches, including from the United and Independent churches and those from the Orthodox, Anglican, Baptist, Lutheran, Methodist, and Reformed faith traditions. While the Roman Catholic Church is not an official member of the WCC, many Roman Catholics have always been on staff with the WCC.

At the founding of the WCC at its first Assembly in Amsterdam in 1948, most of the initial 147 represented churches were from Europe and North America; currently, however, Africa, Asia, the Caribbean, Latin America, the Middle East, and the Pacific encompass a far greater number. With its administrative offices in Geneva, and representing over 560 million Christians, the WCC has as its primary mission to seek Christian unity and bear witness through service. Major themes of the council's work are related to such areas as unity, mission, evangelism, and spirituality; public witness; addressing power and affirming peace; justice, *diakonia*, and responsibility toward creation; education and ecumenical formation; and interreligious dialogue and cooperation.[7]

Vatican II and Beyond

While the early modern-day ecumenical efforts were largely dominated by Protestant leadership and participation, with little Catholic involvement, that changed when 76-year-old Angelo Giuseppe Roncalli (1881–1963) was elected to become Pope John XXIII in 1958. With his calling for the Second Vatican Council (1962–5), John XXIII famously expressed that the Church was in need to open its windows to allow fresh air to enter in with what he called *aggiornamento* (bringing up to date). He sought a modern-age Church renewal not only to better connect with its people but also to promote interfaith and interreligious dialogue. Indeed, observers from other faith traditions were invited to the council to participate in the promotion for unity and healing.[8]

A major document that emerged out of Vatican II is titled *Unitatis Redintegratio* (Decree on Ecumenism) (1964), which harkens to the aforementioned words of Jesus, "so that they may all be one, as you, Father, are in me and I in you, that they also may be in us, that the world may believe that you sent me."[9] The beginning of the report established a principal trajectory of the entire council: "The restoration of unity among all Christians is one of the principal concerns of the Second Vatican Council … This movement toward unity is called 'ecumenical.'"[10]

The term "ecumenical" comes from the Latin *oecumenicus* (general, universal), from the Greek words *oikoumenikos* (from the whole world) and *oikos* (house), which formed into an ecclesiastical word in bringing together, in particular, the Christian community, a universality of a unified presence despite differences.[11] *Unitatis Redintegratio* is laced with a spirit of humility, a sense of fostering dialogue and goodwill, and places a keen value on living a life of holiness not only as individuals but also as corporate bodies, recognizing the nurturing of unity is framed through the engagement in public and private prayer, which is "regarded as the soul of the whole ecumenical movement, and merits the name, 'spiritual ecumenism.'"[12]

In October 2016, on the eve of the 500th-year anniversary of the Protestant Reformation, Pope Francis traveled to heavily Lutheran populated Sweden to celebrate the ecumenical event. A few months earlier, Francis had recognized Martin Luther not only as an intelligent man who had rightly called out the corruption that was within the Church but also as a great reformer.[13] This is a significant acknowledgment, as the Reformation led to years of bitter, violent, and even deadly skirmishes between Catholics and Protestants (and among Protestants themselves); therefore, to witness where we are today as a result of the ecumenical movement is historically remarkable.

And while Lutherans and Catholics still have theological differences, the relationship between the two churches is cemented by a spiritual ecumenism through the cultivation of a mutually gracious ongoing dialogical exchange.[14] In fact, with Protestants in general, and with the variety of denominations therein, ecumenical progress has not only continued in their relationship with the Catholic Church but also among Protestant themselves, particularly since the 1910 Edinburgh Conference, the formation of the WCC, and Vatican II.

In addition to the spiritual ecumenism that has unfolded between Catholics and Protestants, this spirit has also been infused between Protestants and the Orthodox churches through the World Council of Churches and other assemblies, and infused between Catholics and Orthodox churches. In 1964, Pope Paul VI and Ecumenical Patriarch Athenagoras I of Constantinople met in Jerusalem, the first time the Catholic head from the Western Church met with the spiritual head of the Eastern Church since the Council of Florence in 1438.[15] Later, in 1965, both Pope Paul VI and Patriarch Athenagoras expressed regret regarding the simultaneous sentences of excommunication of Pope Leo IX and Patriarch Cerularius, which led to the 1054 Great Schism (see Appendix A). Indeed, John XXIII, Paul VI, and subsequent popes have prioritized an ecumenical bond with Orthodox churches, as both traditions share common aspects of liturgical and sacramental practices.

Interfaith and Interreligious Dialogue

Ecumenism, as mentioned earlier, is associated with unifying relationships among varying Christian groups. However, a necessary furthering of coming to common understandings among religious groups—particularly in light of building a more peaceful and loving civil society—is interreligious and interfaith interaction (or dialogue), the channel that allows us "to swim alongside each other."[16] While the concepts interfaith and interreligious are often used interchangeably, the Archdiocese of Chicago provides a useful distinction between the two. For the former, interfaith suggests relationships among the "Abrahamic faiths" (Christian, Jewish, and Moslem traditions), and for the latter, interreligious suggests relationships among other religions (e.g., Hinduism and Buddhism).[17]

In that light, another landmark document that emerged from Vatican II was *Nostra Aetate* (In Our Age), issued by Pope Paul VI in October 1965, a couple of months before the close of the council. *Nostra Aetate* underscores the importance of dialogical exchanges with other religions, including making clear the denunciation of anti-Semitism and rejecting the charge that the Jews were guilty for the crucifixion of Jesus. Because of Christianity's historical complicity in anti-Semitism, at times quite violently, this document significantly contributed to a healing path between the two faith traditions.[18] This historic report closes with its final paragraph, exhorting,

> The Church reproves, as foreign to the mind of Christ, any discrimination against men or harassment of them because of their race, color, condition of life, or religion. On the contrary, following in the footsteps of the holy Apostles Peter and Paul, this sacred synod ardently implores the Christian faithful to "maintain good fellowship among the nations" (1 Peter 2:12), and, if possible, to live for their part in peace with all men [Romans 12:18], so that they may truly be sons of the Father who is in heaven [Matthew 5:45].[19]

During his pontificate, Pope John Paul II not only claimed ecumenism as an important function of the Church, particularly through his 1995 encyclical *Ut Unum Sint* (That They Be One), but he also emphasized interfaith and interreligious dialogue throughout his pontificate.[20] In an historic moment in 1986, as the first pope in recorded history to visit a synagogue in an official capacity, John Paul II went to Rome's Great Synagogue to continue the work to mend the relationship between Catholics and Jews. During that visit he embraced his Jewish brethren as "older brothers" and strongly reiterated the condemnation of anti-Semitism, announcing, "Yes, once again, through me, the Church, with the words of the well-known decree *Nostra Aetate*, 'deplores the hatred, persecutions and all manifestations of anti-Semitism directed against the Jews at all times by anyone'; I repeat: 'by anyone.'"[21] Pope Benedict also visited Rome's Great Synagogue in 2010, as did Pope Francis in 2016, both of whom iterated the commitment to interreligious dialogue and comradery.

In addition to the prioritization of building a genuine relationship between Christians and Jews, the Church has also been acutely vigilant in fostering meaningful dialogical exchanges with Muslims. *Nostra Aetate* states,

> The Church regards with esteem also the Moslems. They adore the one God, living and subsisting in Himself … They take pains to submit wholeheartedly to even His inscrutable decrees, just as Abraham, with whom the faith of Islam takes pleasure in linking itself, submitted to God. Though they do not acknowledge Jesus as God, they revere Him as a prophet. They also honor Mary, His virgin Mother; at times they even call on her with devotion … Since in the course of centuries not a few quarrels and hostilities have arisen between Christians and Moslems, this sacred synod urges all to forget the past and to work sincerely for mutual understanding and to preserve as well as to promote together for the benefit of all mankind social justice and moral welfare, as well as peace and freedom.[22]

On October 3, 2020, at the tomb of St. Francis (1181 or 1182–1226), the evening before his feast day, Pope Francis released his encyclical

Fratelli Tutti (all brothers and sisters).[23] Arguably the best-known saint of the Catholic Church and one who transcends political, geographic religious, and cultural differences, Francis embraced the idea of pluralism (brothers and sisters we are all) and respect for the planet (Mother Earth, Brother Sun, Sister Moon).[24] Early on in *Fratelli Tutti*, Pope Francis recalls the date 1219 when St. Francis visited with Sultan Malik-el-Kamil in Egypt in an effort to find common ground, despite difference in religious traditions and cultural context. In the midst of the era of the Crusades, what Francis of Assisi was attempting to do was historic and has left a lasting impression on both Muslims and Christians.

Following in the footsteps of St. Francis, Pope Francis has continued on with the ongoing mending of the relationship between Muslims and Christians with an historic visit to Iraq in March 2021. Despite being in the throes of a worldwide Covid-19 pandemic, within a journey of heightened security risks, this first-ever papal trip to the birthplace of Abraham, the patriarchal father of Islam, Judaism, and Christianity, was one in which the Pope came as a "pilgrim of peace" to extend a hand of reconciliation. In addition to providing a significant boost to the minority, beleaguered Christian community in Iraq, he met with the Grand Ayatollah al-Sistani, a principal figure in Shi'ite Islam and a prominent religious authority in Iraq. Indeed, a central focus for the trip was not so much to dwell on differences and conflict but rather one to find ways to dialogue, unite, heal, and reconcile.[25]

Ecumenism and the Laity

Responding to the exhortation of Jesus that we look to be one as a Christian community, and particularly since Vatican II, considerable strides have been made through official church proclamation and clerical action. And this ecumenical activism categorically extends to the laity, a term that comes from the Greek *laikos* (Latin, *laicus*), denoting "of or from the people."[26] Indeed, another notable document that emerged from Vatican II, *Lumen Gentium* (Light for the Nations), affirms the imperative role of the laity and their vocation of family, social, and work life in which all "are called in a special way to make the Church present and operative in those places and circumstances where only through them can it become the salt of the earth."[27]

It is in the Gospel of Matthew 5:13-16 where Jesus reminds his listeners to be the "salt of the earth" and to be the "light of the world," and it is in Paul's letter to the Colossians 4:6 where he exhorts Christians to season their speech with salt. And in the context of the theme of this chapter, therefore, in the effort to create more loving, just, and understanding spaces in a world that is populated with religious, racial, cultural, social, economic, and geographic differences, it is a mandate for the individual Christian to realize that a necessary function of the Church (the people) is sprinkling one's life, speech, and action with a salt of gentleness and an embracing light that looks to promote ecumenism and to foster interfaith and interreligious relationships.

And it is that promotion that makes possible the inclusive umbrella aspect of the Catholic Church with all the good that it does around the world working with diverse peoples with its missions, charity work, hospitals, and schools.

An Inclusive Umbrella That Is the Church

*Being the Church, to be the People of God, in accordance with the
Father's great design of love, means to be the leaven of God in this
humanity of ours.*

Pope Francis, 2013

In the mid-1980s I had the privilege, along with 10,000 other people,
of hearing Mother Teresa (1910–97) speak at a convocation in New
Orleans. While standing only five feet tall and weighing approximately
100 pounds, Mother Teresa spoke with authority, yet with a palpable
humility, captivating the entire arena. To listen to her was to realize
holiness in the midst, of a saint who lived throughout much of the
twentieth century and was deeply admired by those in and out of the
Church. She was officially canonized a saint by Pope Francis in 2016.

At the age of eighteen, the then Gonxha Agnes felt a call to become a
missionary and left her homeland of Albania (now Macedonia) to join
the Sisters of Loreto in Ireland, where she received her new name, Sister
Mary Teresa. This name was given after St. Thérèse of Lisieux (1873–
97), often referred to as "Little Flower," who, through the simplicity of
her life and way of being, has profoundly touched the spirituality of
millions from around the world. It was shortly after her First Profession
of vows in 1931 that Sister Mary Teresa was assigned to teach at St.
Mary's School for girls in Calcutta.[1]

Later, in 1937, she made her Final Profession of Vows, commencing
to use what became her well-recognized name Mother Teresa. She
continued her work in education, becoming the school principal at
St. Mary's, living a life of deep prayer as an integral member of the Sisters

of Loreto. During this time period, in 1946, Mother Teresa received a "call within a call" that would dramatically change her life and the lives of so many others.[2]

Leaving behind her membership as a Sister of Charity, Mother Teresa established the Missionaries of Charity in 1950, shining a spotlight on the "poorest of the poor," as her congregation of sisters, many of whom were her former students, looked to bring dignity, hope, love, and nurturance to the poor, sick, and dying on the streets of Calcutta. As the acceptance of, popularity of, and need for her work grew, Mother Teresa sent her sisters to other parts of India, and still later the Missionaries of Charity spread to other parts of the world, including the establishment of the Missionaries of Charity Brothers, the Missionaries of Charity of Fathers, and the Lay Missionaries of Charity.[3]

For her inspirational efforts, Mother Teresa, among numerous other recognitions, was awarded the 1979 Nobel Peace Prize. At her acceptance speech, she shared the following thoughts:

> To this love for one another and today when I have received this reward, I personally am most unworthy, and I having avowed poverty to be able to understand the poor, I choose the poverty of our people. But I am grateful and I am very happy to receive it in the name of the hungry, of the naked, of the homeless, of the crippled, of the blind, of the leprous, of all those people who feel unwanted, unloved, uncared, thrown away of the society, people who have become a burden to the society, and are ashamed by everybody. In their name I accept the award.[4]

Motivated by a benevolent love for humanity, sustained with a deep faith in the God of love, and indelibly recognized for the traditional white sari with three blue borders,[5] Mother Teresa's ministry was one in which she sought not only to feed and clothe but also to impart dignity, honor, and love to the poor, regardless of race, ethnicity, caste, or creed.

Central to her idea of spreading the Gospel message was not so much through words but through action, in demonstration. St. Francis of Assisi is quoted as saying, "Preach the Gospel always, and if necessary, use words."[6] The goal of the Missionaries of Charity is not to impose the Catholic faith; rather, it is to nurture an active faith that focuses on respect for all religions, and when one finds God, "It is for you to do what God wants you to do."[7] This way of interreligious thinking and doing manifests the inclusive umbrella of the Catholic Church as a welcoming presence in its service for a diverse, multicultural world.

Fostering Diversity

Regarding diversity, particularly as it relates to African Americans and the Catholic Church, we must highlight a beautiful soul named Sister Thea Bowman (1937–90), a member of the Franciscan Sisters of Perpetual Adoration. A few years before my convocation attendance to hear Mother Teresa, I had attended a Catholic Conference in Denver, Colorado, where Sister Thea—as she was affectionately called—was a featured speaker. Her charismatic oratorical skills and her heavenly choir singing voice easily drew one in. And beneath those gifts, most importantly, a clear love for God radiated her empowering presence for the Church, and more specifically, for the Black community.

As a granddaughter of slaves and an only child of a mother who was a teacher and a father who was a physician, Sister Thea, a native Mississippian, was dedicated to the cause of civil rights, particularly as a Black Catholic and the only African American in her religious order in a church that had an initially hesitant response to the Civil Rights Movement. Naturally, it was important to her not to only work toward a more just, right, equitable, and loving world but also to educate, more than rhetorically asking,

> What does it mean to be Black and Catholic? It means that I come to my Church fully functioning. That doesn't frightened you, does it? ... I bring myself, my Black self. All that I am. All that I have. All that I hope to become. I bring my whole history, my traditions, my experience, my culture, my African American song and dance and gesture and movement and teaching and preaching and healing and responsibility as gift to the church.[8]

As an important voice for the Black Catholic experience and a founding faculty member for Black Catholic studies at Xavier University in New Orleans (a program still fully operational to this day), Sister Thea follows in the legacy of Mother Katherine Drexel (1858–1955), the foundress of the Sisters of the Blessed Sacrament, who in 1915 opened a high school that particularly ministered to African Americans and Native Americans. This school added a Normal School (i.e., an institution for teacher education) and eventually became to what it is today, Xavier University of New Orleans.[9]

Drexel was canonized a Saint by Pope John Paul II (1920–2005) in 2000, and there is a formal cause in motion for Sister Thea Bowman to be canonized. To be sure, Mother Katherine Drexel and Sister Thea Bowman, through their work and commitment alongside other notable Black Catholics, have contributed to forming a powerful collective voice of conscience for the Catholic Church as it continues its mission to foster diversity within the warm human embrace of inclusivity.[10]

To Care, to Feed, and to Walk in Courage

Expressing that inclusivity spirit, through what is described as "theology of accompaniment," Dr. Paul Farmer (1959–2002),[11] founder of Partners in Health (PIH), had tirelessly worked to bring health care to the poor at his medical clinic in rural Haiti. A devout Catholic, Farmer, along with the renowned Peruvian theologian Gustavo Gutiérrez, views a theology of accompaniment as a way of thinking and doing.[12] In the introduction of the book *In the Company of the Poor: Conversations with Dr. Paul Farmer and Gustavo Gutiérrez*, Jennie Weiss Block and Michael Griffin describe this theology in the following way:

> The practice of accompaniment is highly personal and deeply relational. Accompaniment of the lonely poor involves walking with—not behind or in front—but beside a real person on his or her own particular journey in his or her own particular place and time, at his or her own particular pace. Accompanying others in their struggles for survival

does not have a beginning or an end, and there is no outside plan to be imposed ... Accompaniment, the act of 'walking with another' is, in the words of Roberto Goizueta, 'always a fundamentally religious sacramental act.'[13]

Through this sacramental act, under the inclusive umbrella of the Catholic Church, this practice of accompaniment embraces the real person along the journey of life from right where he or she may be, without imposing but simply by being there in the person of Dr. Paul Farmer and his associates.

Consider also the humanitarian work of world-famous chef José Andrés, who formed World Central Kitchen (WCK). In response to humanitarian, climate, and community crises, WCK works—in conjunction with local communities—to feed and care for the hungry, realizing food is a universal human right. Whether these crises occur in Brazil, Puerto Rico, Haiti, Australia, Lebanon, the United States, or any number of countries, WCK looks to respond to John Steinbeck's sentiment, "Wherever there's a fight so that hungry people may eat ... we'll be there."[14] In fact, at the moment of this writing, Chef Andrés and his team are in Ukraine within the midst of the horrible Russian-Ukraine conflict. And the cornerstone of Andrés motivation is his Catholic faith; he asserts, "My faith has a lot to do with my life ... I was raised in a Catholic family that was always helping and feeding people ... As a little boy going to religious classes, I thought Jesus was so cool. He could do so much like make breakfast for fisherman. Jesus cooked it himself."[15]

We should reflect in awe at the bravery of Sister Ann Nu Thawng, who, as a member of the Sisters of Francis Xavier, bravely kneeled before heavily armored riot police in Myanmar, begging for the shooting of protesters to stop.[16] The captivating photo of the sister's bold act spread throughout the world, as she reportedly declared to the riot police, "You'll have to come through me. Shoot me instead of these young people."[17] Because of a brutal military repression beginning in February 2021, protestors took to the streets only to face gun fire that, as of this writing, has already killed over 1,000 civilians, with many who have been injured, along with over 2,000 detainees. The president of the Catholic Bishops Conference of Myanmar, Cardinal Charles Maung Bo, condemned the violence, urging that the people had a right to peacefully gather.[18] Pope Francis echoed the Cardinal's sentiments, and exclaimed, "I, too, kneel on the streets of Myanmar and say, 'Stop the violence … I, too, spread wide my arms and say, Make way for dialogue.'"[19] Sister Ann Nu Thawng's singular brave act was instrumental in shining a bright light on what was happening in Myanmar, which has contributed to saving lives, cultivating some semblance of hope within the midst of terrorizing acts.

The lives and works of Mother Teresa, Sister Thea Bowman, Mother Katherine Drexel, Dr. Paul Farmer, José Andrés, and Sister Ann Nu Thawng are only but a few—relatively contemporary—examples, among countless known and unknown others, throughout the history of the Church—who have put a human face on the embracing inclusivity and goodness of the Church. Without that embrace, the world would be less lovely, less hopeful, less beautiful. It is indeed the lives and work of such individuals that also comprise the various Church-associated organizations in which its presence is manifested around the world.

Working Hands of Women Religious and Others

Consider also the combined work of women religious who have historically been a force of goodness, justice, and love with their presence. Women religious have made a professed vow of chastity, poverty, and obedience and taken on a role to be either a sister or a nun. While those two terms are often used interchangeably, a "sister" is one who more commonly lives out her vocation in a public fashion (teaching, hospital work, missions, etc.), whereas a "nun" generally lives a cloistered life in a monastery or convent.[20] Either way, there is a deep love for God and a deep commitment to the welfare of people.

In a very real way women religious can be considered the first feminists, particular in the era where women were not encouraged to work outside the home. In contrast, women religious held managing positions in hospitals, schools, charitable organizations, and schools. During the US Civil War (1861–5), women religious were a critical presence, providing much needed nursing skills to both sides of the conflict. Later, in 1900s, they were responsible for building the largest private school system and hospital systems, and still later, they were instrumental in activating the Church during the Civil Rights Movement. And while Bill Wilson and Dr. Bob Smith are more commonly recognized for the founding of Alcoholics Anonymous (AA), a highly effective international program to assist the maintaining of sobriety, Sister Ignatia Gavin of the Sisters of Charity was also a founding member. She tirelessly worked to open the doors of hospital care for those who needed treatment for alcoholism.[21]

But, of course, women religious orders have made their presence known all over the world. Whether it is the Maryknoll Sisters, who founded seven hospitals and seventeen schools, making God's love visible by serving the poor and marginalized as doctors, social workers, teachers, theologians, environmentalists, and nurses (https://www.maryknollsisters.org/), or the Little Sisters of the Poor, whose central mission is to care for the elderly poor, regardless of race or religion (https://littlesistersofthepoor.org/), or the Sisters of Mercy, who focus on works of mercy to feed the hungry, clothed the naked, visit the sick, and comfort the afflicted, along with other spiritual and corporal works of mercy in an effort to better the world (https://www.sistersofmercy.org/), these are but only three among numerous examples in which women religious orders have demonstrated love and care for humanity in their own unique, embracing way.

To be sure, like women religious, there are numerous religious orders for men leading lives that demonstrate the inclusive warm embrace of the Church. In addition, there are many other Catholic organizations such as Catholic Charities, Catholic Relief Services, Caritas Internationalis, and so many others around the world doing impactful work similar to that of religious orders. In the end, as one examines the presence of the Church around the world, it is—as highlighted with a few examples here—the human face, the warm touch, and gentle smile that powerfully manifest that presence. This, I believe, is relevant for the Catholic teacher to recognize.

Furthering the Legacy

As the Catholic teacher reflects on her vocation, it is necessary not only to possess a basic understanding of the Church's rich history and its imperative to be engaged in ecumenical, interreligious, and interfaith dialogue but also to warmly appreciate and even be inspired by the legacy of so many who have exemplified the inclusive umbrella that is the Church. In this way, the Catholic teacher can better contextualize her work and the nature of her vocation as a "means to be the leaven of God" in the furthering of that legacy.[22]

Teaching as a Vocation

Only the brave should teach …. Teaching is a vocation. It is as sacred as priesthood; as innate as desire, as inescapable as the genius which compels a great artist.

Pearl Buck, 1950

One of the prayers included in the order of a Catholic Mass is called the Universal Prayer (also called Prayer of the Faithful) where the minister (often a congregant) will lead the gathering through a prayer of petitions or intentions (e.g., specific needs for the Church, church officials, government leaders, peace in the world, etc.). In my experience, since I was a child wherever or whenever I went to Mass, a common petition always generally included is to pray for more vocations in the church, explicitly or implicitly meaning to the priesthood or the religious life.[1]

Growing up Catholic before the realization of the tangible implications of Vatican II, it was somehow conveyed to me (and my siblings and peers) that becoming a priest or joining a religious community was the ultimate path to holiness—so I thought, so many of us thought (and perhaps some still do).[2] While for many years I seriously contemplated becoming a Catholic priest, I never received the call.

"Vocation" is a term that has its roots in the Latin *vocare*, meaning "to call" or to summon. Among Catholic circles, therefore, particularly for those who are formally leaning toward the religious life, the language or thought that is used during that discernment process is whether one senses the call or the summons to enter that way of life. However, over the last sixty years, the concept of vocation has thankfully become more comprehensive in its intent, as have the variety of paths therein to do God's will and reach communion with the Divine.

We also learned from Chapter 2 of Vatican II documents affirming the role of the laity and their necessary place within the apostolate of the Church. In that light, another church document that emerged from Vatican II, *Gravissimum Educationis* (Declaration of Christian Education) (1965), underscores that education is an inalienable universal right for all, emphasizing the importance of schools and highlighting teaching as a vocation that "demands special qualities of mind and heart, very careful preparation, and continuing readiness to renew and adapt."[3]

A monograph titled *The Vocation of the Catholic Educator* notes that while Catholic educators must obviously possess expertise in the field, the work is more than a job; it is a "divine calling," a vocation, in which their interaction with students must be one that reflects a living witness of the faith. Authored by Richard M. Jacobs, a Catholic priest with the Augustinian order, this monograph was released in 1996 by the National Catholic Education Association and is particularly geared for Catholic educators working in Catholic schools; yet, it surely has universal appeal whether or not the Catholic educator is working in a Catholic school: that is, to become a teacher is indeed—as Pearl Buck suggests at the onset of this chapter—a vocation in which one is beckoned by a divine calling.[4]

In fact, over a decade before Jacobs's publication, the Sacred Congregation for Catholic Education published *Lay Catholics in Schools: Witnesses to Faith* (1982), which states that the work of the lay Catholic educator must not be reduced to teaching as a profession; rather, it is a "super-natural Christian vocation" and one "that every lay Catholic educator become fully aware of the importance, the richness, and the responsibility of this vocation."[5] The document goes on to emphasize that the Catholic educator has a marked responsibility to communicate truth, to realize the dignity of every human being as a child of God, to possess a keen sense of civic and political responsibility, particularly when it comes to matters related to hunger, illiteracy, and human exploitation, and to build what Pope Paul VI calls a "civilization of love."[6]

Moreover, Catholic educators must inculcate in their students civic and social responsibility so that they, too, will embrace social commitment and solidarity for the other. Finally, the *Lay Catholics in Schools* document underscores that Catholic educators should be those who incorporate a pedagogical approach that cultivates authentic relationships with their students through openness and dialogue that "will facilitate an understanding of the witness to faith that is revealed through the behaviour of the teacher."[7]

In the final analysis, teaching—assuming one takes the serious nature of its work and views personal and professional life through the prism of faith—is a vocation to which one is called, whether working in a Catholic school, public school, or some other non-sectarian school setting. And, regardless of the setting, a fundamental exhibition of that vocation is illuminated through a word-and-deed behavior pattern that exhibits a sense of faith, hope, and love in and for their students and their families, through a place of humility in a pedagogical approach immersed in compassion and persistence.[8]

Of course, because the vocation of the Catholic teacher working in a Catholic school is delineated as a mission to serve the Church, to share the Gospel message, to build the body of Christ, and to be a knowledgeable and skilled professional in the endeavor of serving students, the expression of that vocation takes on a different meaning from that understood by their counterparts working in a public or some other non-sectarian setting. Indeed, there is much literature regarding the role of Catholic teachers and Catholic schools, some of which has been underscored here.[9]

This book, therefore, is not so much an effort to specifically add to that collection of literature, as it were; rather, the hope is that—whether teaching in a public or private school setting—this text will contribute more universally as Catholic teachers (and other educators of faith) realize the vision of their vocation as one that is "beyond solely Catholic school formation and Church affiliation."[10] In other words, the vocation is viewed in a space that looks to the "global compact on education" in which, as Pope Francis emphasizes, education is viewed as a seed of hope toward beauty, goodness, justice, collaboration, solidarity, and social harmony where all human persons are viewed with dignity and respect and have access to a quality education.[11]

And a critical pathway to live out that vocation—one that is mindful of the global impact on education—is to recognize the relevance of personalist thought and to be aware of the social teachings of the Church in which liberation theology is intimately linked through a critical pedagogy in the light of faith lens, all of which are the themes in Section II.

Section II

Know What Informs You: Personalism, Social Teachings of the Church, Liberation Theology, and a Critical Pedagogy in the Light of Faith

Looking through a Personalist Lens

The biggest challenge of the day is: how to bring about a revolution of the heart, a revolution that has to start with each one of us?

Dorothy Day, 1963

As the Catholic teacher comes to appreciate the richness of the "catholic" ecclesial history, the importance of fostering ecumenicalism, interfaith, and interreligious relationships, and the good work people do the world over in the name of the Church, s/he ought to have a sense of pride about how their vocation is framed within a rich heritage. The living out that vocation demands a contemplative way of living (see Chapter 15) and assumes that the personal and professional life of the Catholic teacher is in a continuous unfolding motion, whereby "To be, one must be becoming."[1] In other words, the idea of our becoming recognizes our unfinishedness in the journey of living out the faith, which I believe must be viewed through a personalist lens, as will be highlighted in this chapter.

Among many who have been deeply influenced by Francis of Assisi was Peter Maurin (1877–1949), founder of the Catholic Worker Movement in the 1930s. With its presence still active today, the Catholic Worker Movement (along with their periodical *The Catholic Worker*) remains committed to justice, nonviolence, and ministering to the poor. Although Maurin was the founder, it was Dorothy Day (1897–1980) who has famously placed an enduring face on the movement. Day not only made clear that Maurin would remind followers that Francis of Assisi was the model of inspiration but also that Maurin introduced the movement to the French philosopher Emmanuel Mounier (1905–50) and his concept of personalism.[2] Even taking it further, Day declared that Francis of Assisi "was most truly the 'great personalist.'"[3]

While the existentialism of Jean-Paul Sartre (1889–1973) focused on the individualism of personhood, Mounier, naturally drawing from existential and phenomenological thought coupled with the influence of his Catholic faith, promoted a personalism, which looked to the interiority of the person, the spiritual being in which human beings are active subjects of history.

In short, the centrality of the person, the uniqueness of personhood, and the relational intersection of persons are fundamental to personalist thought.[4] Thus, for Mounier, the person as a spiritual being, acting as subject, implies that one is not an object but rather exists through action moving the subjective self from the center in order to realize that purposeful existence occurs through relationships with others.[5] Similarly, Pope Francis, who employs a personalist lens, states, "Each of us is fully a person when we are part of a people; at the same time, there are no peoples without respect for the individuality of each person."[6]

In other words, unlike individualism, which essentially is a philosophy of isolation and self-absorption,[7] the concept of personalism, while realizing the self in personhood, involves a constant dynamic to move outside of self to provide access to the challenges that cause human beings to struggle and thus work toward "humanizing" humanity.[8] Peter Roberts, philosopher of education at the University of Canterbury, New Zealand, expands the point:

> The vocation of becoming more fully human is what defines us as human beings; it is the *essence* of being human. Humanization is an historical, as well as ontological, vocation because it calls us to act (on the basis of critical reflection) in the objective world of lived social relations. Dehumanization represents a distortion of this vocation.[9]

While existentialism can tend to come from a depressed, anxiety-filled disposition centrally focused on interior development as the basic purpose of existence, personalism emerges fundamentally as a humanist philosophy. That is, human beings are not determinant but rather the centrality of the person as subject is the beginning point for ontological and epistemological reflection. As such, one acts as a participant in life rather than as a spectator and in participative relationships with others, critically examining the dignity, status, and experience of what it means to be human.[10]

Mounier's response to early twentieth-century European economic, social, and institutional religion turmoil was the antithesis of Nietzsche's notion of "God is dead" and that religion was for the weak or Marx's assertion of religion being the "opium of the people." While clearly recognizing that class struggle and economic inequities were real, Mounier did not view that utopia (or the ideal) would be found in simply finding the solution to economic realities, nor was the solution to be found in the political establishment and the traditional church. Rather, seeking to reinvent the Church and French society, Mounier was looking for a more authentic revitalization or revolution of a new humanism in which the bourgeois would yield to an authentic Christianity, suggesting a lived faith renewed in community and in which there was a denunciation of the old,[11] and a move toward growing the Kingdom of God in which "the new man is therefore called upon to make a new earth and the world of the body is asked to put forth its strength, not merely to declare the glory of God, but also to create it."[12]

Informed by Humanist Thought

Mounier's idea of personalism is informed by a humanist philosophy in which he argued that "humanism is a will to totality," suggesting there is a oneness or a reuniting of "body and spirit, meditation and operation, thought and action."[13] For Mounier, spirituality is that deeper part of oneself, meaning that human civilization or culture cannot exist apart from the metaphysical.

That is, "Only a program that looks beyond effort and production, a science that looks beyond utility, an art that looks beyond agreement, and finally a personal life devoted to a spiritual reality that carries each one beyond himself—are capable of lifting the weight of a dead past and giving birth to a truly new order."[14] To that end, for Mounier, Christian humanism rests in Divine generosity. Despite the reality of human suffering that exists and the paradoxical nature that life can be, Mounier characterizes his perspective as "tragic optimism," as opposed to a pessimism that drives some humanist thought.[15]

Although evidence of a humanist philosophy can be traced back earlier, the generally accepted origination of modern humanism can be dated back to the fourteenth century, during the era of the European Renaissance, where the concepts of individualism, worth, thought, capacity, dignity, and human concern were emphasized as opposed to the religious or theological thinking that had driven perspective and interpretation of reality.[16] Like personalism, humanism can be challenging to define concretely because over time multiple perspectives have driven its meaning, in addition to broadly splitting into secular and spiritual or religious (see endnote 4 for this chapter).

Broadly, on the one hand, the foundation of secular humanism remains rooted in the thinking of the Enlightenment (i.e., Descartes's "I think, therefore I am"), depending on the evidence of empirical science, and rejects the supernatural, looking to the wisdom of individuals in the move toward a more just social reality and the common good.[17] And, on the other hand, juxtaposed to the secular nature of humanist philosophy, the theologian Karl Barth (1886–1968) argued that authentic humanism is not possible without the infusion of the Gospel message as its foundation. Moreover, Jacques Maritain (1882–1973), a Neo–Thomist strongly influenced by the philosopher Henri Bergson (1859–1941), argued for what he characterized as "integral humanism," making the point that a humanism lacking a spiritual dimension would amount to a partial humanism.[18]

Thus, authentic humanism necessarily "integrates" the spiritual as a critical aspect into the description of what it means to be a whole person, reflecting the views of Mounier and other Christian thinkers such as Teilhard de Chardin (1881–1955) and Karl Rahner (1904–84). And while there is naturally a distinct foundational difference between secular and Christian humanism (and other strands of humanism), all humanist thought is fundamentally grounded in a love for life, is socially conscious, takes responsibility, seeks to explore new knowledge and discover new adventures, and works to ascertain solutions to human problems and challenges.[19]

Implications for the Catholic Teacher

For personalists, there is a distinct difference between persons and non-persons; there is an exceptionalism of the human person from all other life forms. This exceptionalism not only suggests that human beings are more than matter, more than an animal, and distinctly different from animals but also that every human being is unique unto himself; a person is a "somebody," not a "something," a "subject," not an "object."[20] To cite the poem "I Am—Somebody" by civil rights activist Reverend William Holmes Borders, Sr. (1905–93), personalism stresses the significance of community and the "somebodiness" of each individual in that community.[21]

Like Dorothy Day, Pope John Paul II, and Martin Luther King, Jr., among others, who viewed their ministries through a personalist lens, Catholic teachers would be well served by doing the same in their vocation. Persistently mindful of the "somebodiness" of each student in the class, even of the parents/guardians of students, along with colleagues, this not only places the humanity of the other at the forefront of thought but also works as a reminder that each of us has a story.

Each of our stories is unique to us, meaning, regardless of race, culture, religion, gender, or economic standing, all of us are equals deserving of respect and dignity. And the engendering of that respect and dignity unfolds in the nurturing of relationships. Worthwhile to cite at length, Pope Francis further affirms the point:

> I cannot know myself apart from a broader network of relationships, including those that have preceded me and shaped my entire life. My relationship with those whom I respect has to take account of the fact

that they do not live only for me, nor do I live only for them. Our relationships, if healthy and authentic, open us to others who expand and enrich us ... By its very nature, love calls for growth in openness and the ability to accept others as part of a continuing adventure that makes every periphery converge in a great sense of mutual belonging. As Jesus told us: "You are all brothers" (Mt. 23:8) ... Social friendship and universal fraternity necessarily call for an acknowledgement of *the worth of every human person*, always and everywhere [author's emphasis] ... The world exists for everyone, because all of us were born with the same dignity. Differences of colour, religion, talent, place of birth or residence, and so many others, cannot be used to justify the privileges of some over the rights of all. As a community, we have an obligation to ensure that every person lives with dignity and has sufficient opportunities for his or her integral development.[22]

The obligation to ensure the worth and dignity of every human person should prompt the Catholic teacher to enter into communion with their students and others in what the Jewish personalist Martin Buber (1878–1965) calls an *I and thou* relationship as opposed to an *I-it* relationship pattern. The former is driven by a sense of love and respect, illuminated through authentic dialogue in a co-existing relationship between persons; the latter is propelled by the idea that the "I" is the creator of things and manipulator of the other.[23]

The notion of an "it" with respect to relationships situates the other as an object, not only impeding dialogue, but also representing a deformation of education.[24] In the context of education, therefore, the idea of the unfolding of an I-thou relationship functions through a teacher's ability to lovingly, respectively, and intentionally be available and present with her students. That is, the I and the thou suggest we are not alone; we coexist; there is a between with one to another, all of which is an encounter of inclusion.

In the end, viewing the world through a personalist lens takes commitment, which unfolds through what Dorothy Day calls a "revolution of the heart," assuming an understanding of our unfinishedness in the journey of our becoming; this journey recognizes each of us is a unique human being, yet conscious of the other, realizing our purpose flourishes through relationships.[25] And to be intentional about the flourishing of those relationships, particularly when working with students and families from all walks of life and the living out of one's faith in general, it is necessary for the Catholic teacher to possess a basic awareness of the social teachings of the Church.

An Overview of the Social Teachings of the Church

Far too many Catholics are not familiar with the basic content of Catholic social teaching. More fundamentally, many Catholics do not adequately understand that the social teaching of the Church is an essential part of Catholic faith.

United States Conference of Catholic Bishops, 2011

When Jesus set out to begin his public ministry, as was the custom, he went to the synagogue on the Sabbath day in the area where he grew up in Nazareth. He stood up before the congregation and was given the scroll; he unrolled it and read a passage from the prophet Isaiah:

The Spirit of the Lord is upon me, because he has anointed me to bring glad tidings to the poor. He has sent me to proclaim liberty to captives and recovery of sight to the blind, to let the oppressed go free, and to proclaim a year acceptable to the Lord.[1]

Then Jesus rolled the scroll back up, and with the eyes of the congregants keenly focused on him, he pronounced, "Today this scripture passage is fulfilled in your hearing." And all were amazed at the man who was present in their midst.[2] This particular Lukan passage succinctly captures Jesus's salvation mission of love, hope, and justice, a mission that biblically frames the social teachings of the Church.[3]

The God of life is not only interested in a personal relationship with each one of us but also in the communal and social nature of that relationship. We are called to look out for one another, particularly the poor, the marginalized, those that are hurting, and all those on the outside looking in, for whom pumps the life blood of Catholic social teaching. We are all created in the image of God, and thus from conception to the end of our natural lives, all possess a right to life, are inherently valuable, and deserving of dignity.[4]

An Early Example

Bartolomé de Las Casas (1484–1566) stands out as a forerunner, an example, of one who shaped the social teaching documents of the Church. As a young boy in Seville, Spain, Las Casas crossed paths with Christopher Columbus after he returned from his first voyage to the "New World," witnessing the explorer showcasing enslaved members from the Taíno tribe who were brought back. Later, Las Casas's father and three of his uncles joined Columbus on his second voyage.

Still later, in 1507, Las Casas made what was his second voyage across the Atlantic, thereafter becoming the first priest ordained in the "New World." His ordination occurred under the aegis of the Spanish Crown during a disturbing era when dehumanizing colonization was in process and an obsession to find gold and riches by any means necessary was well in place. The indigenous populations, whom the Spanish called "Indians," were enslaved, viewed as less than human, harshly treated, and summarily tortured and killed.[5]

While Las Casas initially freely participated in the *encomienda* or plantation system—with his possession of land and slaves—he was deeply affected by the brutality taking place.[6] This, coupled with his own rereading of Scripture and a deep conversion, led Las Casas to denounce the repression; he gave up ownership of land and freed his own slaves. He joined the Dominican order and devoted the rest of life defending the rights and dignity of the Indians, despite severe opposition and death threats for his steadfast stance.[7] In a powerful piece, Robert Ellsberg, editor-in-chief and publisher of Orbis books, writes that the theological insights of Las Casa went beyond simply affirming the human dignity of the Indians. That is,

> In their sufferings, he argued, the Indians truly represented the crucified Christ. So he [Las Casas] wrote, "I leave in the Indies Jesus Christ, our God, scourged and afflicted and beaten and crucified not once, but thousands of times." For las Casas there could be no salvation in Jesus Christ apart from social justice. Thus, the question was not whether the Indians were to be "saved"; the more serious question was the salvation of the Spanish who were persecuting Christ in his poor. Jesus had said that our eternal fate rests on our treatment of those in need: "I was hungry and you fed me, naked and you clothed me. ... Insofar as you have done these things to the least of my brothers and sisters, you have done them to me" (Mt 25:31-40).[8]

Fundamental to the social teachings of the Church is the life and dignity of the human person, promotion of the common good, protection of human rights, placing the needs of the poor and vulnerable at the forefront of priority (option for the poor), and underscoring solidarity with all those in need.[9] When one examines the life of the Dominican friar who lived 500 years ago, it is clear that as "Protector of the Indians," he placed into action the social teachings of the Church before they were "official" ecclesial documents, and he personified social justice before the term became part of our lexicon.[10]

The Emergence of Church Documents and Vatican II

When Pope Leo XIII (1810–1903) issued his encyclical *Rerum Novarum* (*On the Condition of Workers*) in 1891, he was troubled with the squalid living and working conditions of Europe's urban poor, taking a clear position against the exploitation of the poor "since the great majority of them live undeservedly in miserable and wretched conditions."[11] It was this momentous encyclical in which the "modern" emergence of the social teachings of the Church occurred, laying the foundation for future teachings.[12] Forty years later in 1931, observing the fortieth anniversary of *Rerum Novarum*, Pope Pius XI (1857–1939) released *Quadragesimo Anno* (*On the Fortieth Year*), which spoke out against economic exploitation and unbridled liberal capitalism.[13]

While Leo XIII focused on structural reform, he also concentrated on personal sin and thus called for internal reform. However, Pius XI also viewed sin in a collective sense, arguing that injustice and economic exploitation were committed because of a laissez-faire capitalistic system.[14] After Pope Pius XI, Pope Pius XII (1876–1958) also contributed to the social teachings of the Church, and though he espoused the right of private ownership, he "insisted that this limited right must be subordinate to the interests of the common welfare and the broad right of all people to benefit from the wealth of the earth."[15] These teachings by Popes Leo XII, Pius XI, and Pius XII through the 1950s functioned as the preparation for the social teachings of Pope John XXIII (1881–1963) and Pope Paul VI (1897–1978).

In 1961, Pope John XXIII issued *Mater et Magistra* (*Christianity and Social Progress*), which instructed against any new means of colonialism and exploitation in the form of economic, cultural, and/or political rule. John XXIII argued that property owners should act responsibly and even be compelled by law to do so.[16] With John XXIII convening Vatican II on October 11, 1962, it became clearer, as alluded to in Chapter 2, that this council unexpectedly proved to be one of the most important events in the history of the Church. And with his release of the encyclical *Pacem in Terris* (*Peace on Earth*) during the council, John XXIII emphasized justice, democracy, the common good, religious freedom, human rights, and the elimination of racism.[17] Moreover, Vatican II's *Gaudium et Spes* (*Pastoral Constitution of the Church in the Modern World*) fervently cried out against technological, economic, and political oppression.

In the end, Vatican II shifted the Church from a conservative and authoritarian stance to one that supported political pluralism and social justice, encouraging a more open line of communication with bishops, clergy, laity, and other Christian denominations and religions.[18] A 1967 post-council encyclical by Pope Paul VI, *Populorum Progressio* (*On the Development of Peoples*), focused on world development concerns, with particular attention to raising the quality of life of those who daily confront hunger, poor living conditions, sickness, poor health care, and no opportunity for formal education.

To be sure, subsequent to Vatican II other papal and Vatican documents were released with social justice themes, such as *Octogesima Adveniens* (*A Call to Action*) (Pope Paul VI, 1971), *Sollicitudo Rei Socialis* (*The Concern of the Church for the Social Order*) (Pope John Paul II, 1987), *Evengelium Vitae* (*The Gospel of Life*) (Pope John Paul II, 1995), *Dignitas Personae* (*The Dignity of a Person*) (Congregation for the Doctrine of the Faith, 1998), *Deus Caritas Est* (*God is Love*) (Pope Benedict XVI, 2005), and *Laudato Si* (*On Care for Our Common Home*) (Pope Francis, 2015). In addition to these documents and other church documents from respective countries, the United States Conference of Catholic Bishops has released a host of statements on social justice, with *Economic Justice* (1986) and *A Decade after Economic Justice for All* (1995) being widely influential, among others.[19]

An Essential Part of the Catholic Faith

As implied in the epigraph of this chapter, a basic awareness of the social teachings of the Church is a must for one to live out the dynamism of the Catholic faith, and all the more a charge for the Catholic teacher.[20] Clearly, this chapter has provided an overview of those teachings, which provide an important context for how these teachings grounded the modern emergence of what is known as liberation theology.[21]

An Organic Link to Liberation Theology

God's holiness gives meaning to the work of liberation.

Gustavo Gutiérrez, 1991

When the Argentine Jorge Mario Bergoglio took the name Francis on March 13, 2013, it was clearly more than a symbolic gesture in his becoming the first pope from the Americas. In a personalist spirit and grounded in a deep faith, simplicity, humility, and a love for the poor that guided Francis of Assisi over 800 years ago, Pope Francis has exuded that same charisma throughout his ministry as a Jesuit cleric in Buenos Aires.[1] The thrust of his ministry, seeking a poor Church that possesses a heart for the poor, has patently marked his pontificate. This desire of Francis is not only rooted in the Gospel message but is also the same message that is filtered through Catholic social teaching.

It was thus no great coincidence that only a few months after he assumed the papacy, Francis invited Father Gustavo Gutiérrez to Rome, holding private conversations and concelebrating Mass.[2] It was Gutiérrez's highly influential 1971 book, *A Theology of Liberation*, that provided a groundbreaking critical analysis linking the social, political, and economic conditions of the poor in Latin America in light of theological reflection.

In other words, liberation theology centrally situates the concept of "preferential option for the poor" as its analytical theological starting point, which will be discussed later. After the publication of that landmark work, Gutiérrez released numerous other notable books on faith, theology, and the plight of the poor, recognizing, as stated above, that God's holiness gives meaning to the work.[3] In addition, hundreds of other insightful books on liberation theology have been published over the last sixty years illuminating the organic link between the social teachings of the Church and liberation theology.

Liberation theology, however, has historically been a "thorn in the side" of the institutional church, and while it has not outright rejected the totality of its theological approach, the Church has been more than slightly uncomfortable with theologians viewed as too progressive, as has been the case for Gustavo Gutiérrez.[4] Therefore, the significance of Gutiérrez's meeting with Pope Francis was more than perfunctory; rather, the invitation was an affirming signal to the universal church that a theology of liberation is fundamentally rooted in the Gospel message. Indeed, in the 266th Pontiff, Gutiérrez sees a church with a "change in atmosphere."[5]

In 2020 with his release of *Querida Amazonia (Dear Amazon)*, Pope Francis penned an exhortation to protect the rights, dignity, and land of indigenous populations in the Amazon. Indeed, since the beginning of his pontificate and no doubt familiar with the life and work of Bartolomé de Las Casas, Francis has demonstrated a commitment to indigenous populations throughout the Americas. In 2015, he traveled to Bolivia and offered an historic apology on behalf of the Church for its role in exploitation, colonialism, and the grave sins that "were committed against the native people of America in the name of God." He went further, denouncing a "new colonialism" in which multinational corporations and global capitalism cultivate a system in which materialism is revered, inequality is perpetuated, and exploitation of the poor is painfully evident.[6]

The change in atmosphere that Gutiérrez observed in Pope Francis on behalf of the Church is one that, of course, recognizes the wisdom of the ecclesial social teachings, a wisdom in which Francis incorporates a liberation theology lens; the following section provides a brief historical context.

Historical Context

In 1968 at a conference sponsored by a group of Catholic priests in Chimbote, Peru, Gustavo Gutiérrez gave a presentation for the first what he called "A Theology of Liberation." A few months later, from August 24 to September 6 of that same year, an historic Latin American Bishops' conference took place in Medellín, Colombia. Titled "The Church in the Present-Day Transformation of Latin America in the Light of the Council," the event included the participation of 130 bishops, along with Gutiérrez and other clergy who sought to consider the implications of Vatican II for a Latin American context.[7]

Grounded in the Exodus story of the Hebrew Scriptures and Jesus's first public announcement of bringing "good news to the poor and setting the captives free" (Luke 4), the term "liberation" emerged from Medellín, particularly as a response to unjust economic, agricultural, industrial, cultural, and political realities that clearly violated basic human rights.[8] Moreover, based on the work of the Brazilian educator and philosopher Paulo Freire (1921–97) and his concept of "liberating education," the notion of "participation" was illuminated at the conference. In short, Medellín significantly impacted Latin American politics and in essence dismantled the traditional alliance of the military, the oligarchy, and the Church.[9] While it is beyond the scope of this book to provide a historical description of that alliance, refer to Chapter 6 on the discussion of Bartolomé de Las Casas and also see endnote 6 of the same chapter.

In 1969, at a Commission on Society, Development and Peace (SODEPAX) meeting, jointly sponsored by the World Council of Churches and the Pontifical Commission on Justice and Peace in Cartigny, Switzerland, Gutiérrez gave a presentation similar to the one he had given in Peru the year before. Titled "Notes on a Theology of Liberation," Gutiérrez presented the fundamental framework of liberation theology, ultimately leading to his aforementioned pivotal work, *A Theology of Liberation*. In the contemporary sense of the concept, one could say at this time liberation theology was officially placed on the proverbial world map, leading the theologian Gary Dorrien to assert, "Gustavo Gutiérrez is the most influential figure in modern liberation theology, and arguably the most significant theologian of the past generation. No one has made a greater impact on the shape or direction of theological discussion in our time."[10]

Whereas the Medellín Latin American Bishops' Conference pointedly challenged the social, political, religious, and political establishment, and whereas the Latin American Bishops' Conference of 1979 in Puebla, Mexico, reaffirmed the proposals of Medellín, it was the Puebla conference that most famously introduced the concept of "preferential option for the poor," which was later reaffirmed at the 1992 Latin American bishops' conference in Santo Domingo, and still later in 2007 at the Fifth General Conference of the Bishops of Latin America and the Caribbean in Aparecida, Brazil.[11]

Rooted in Scripture and Prayer

As one examines the thinking and practice of liberation theology, it is clear that following Jesus, a reliance on Scripture, as well as a commitment to prayer is where liberation theology emerges into activism.[12] As in the case of Dom Hélder Câmara (1909–99), who served as Archbishop of Recife and Olinda, Brazil, and who notably contributed to Vatican II. He boldly spoke out on behalf of the poor and called out what liberation theologians refer to as structural or institutional sin (economic, cultural, or social systems that are systemically oppressive). A deeply prayerful man and though he stood just over five feet tall and weighed approximately 120 pounds, Câmara spoke with a commanding, persuasive, passionate voice and was viewed as a threat as he courageously stood up to the Brazilian military dictatorship.[13]

Consider Archbishop Óscar Romero of El Salvador, mentioned in the Preface, who also was a deeply prayerful man and not initially apt to get involved with affairs of the state. Yet, not unlike what happened to Bartolomé de Las Casas, with what can only be considered a profound transformation in light of political corruption and unjust economic and social structures, Romero became a powerful voice on behalf of the poor. At Romero's canonization at St. Peter's Square on October 14, 2018, Pope Francis wore the blood-stained belt that Romero was wearing when he was assassinated.[14]

As evident in their lives, Câmara, Romero, and Las Casas were deeply prayerful men who spiritually grasped the idea, as it says in the epigraph, that it is the holiness of God in which the work of liberation is meaningful. This enabled them to biblically ground their understanding on why a "preferential option for the poor" was a central emphasis of their ministry, the driving focus guiding the thought and actions of liberation theology.

Making a Preferential Option for the Poor

God possesses a preferential option for the poor,[15] not because they are necessarily better than others but simply because they are poor and living in inhumane circumstances; it is in meaningful action toward our neighbor, particularly the poor, that solidarity is intensified and we come in contact with the Lord.[16] In other words, as explained by the theologian Robert McAfee Brown (1920–2002), preferential option does not imply exclusivity, as if God did not love and care for the non-poor; that would not be biblical.[17]

Yet, there is a tendency for some who are wealthy to be threatened by the notion of preferential option, seemingly placing them in a defensive posture. As Brown further elaborates, the poor, because of human greed, patently receive an unfair portion of the world's goods:

> The fact that God does love *all* means that there must be food, shelter, jobs, and humane living conditions for all and not just for some … So for the sake of *all*, and not just for the sake of some, "a preferential option for the poor" provides a guideline for the kinds of change that are necessary to bring greater justice into an unjust world.[18]

The 1986 pastoral letter from the National Conference of Catholic Bishops titled *Economic Justice for All* states "that our faith is tested by the quality of justice among us, that we can best measure our life together by how the poor and the vulnerable are treated."[19] This powerful document suggests that social and economic realities must be viewed from the perspective of the poor and powerless simply because doing so is a response to the biblical imperative to "love thy neighbor as thyself," adding that making a fundamental "option for the poor" is not only a call to consider the common good but also to enable the poor and marginalized to become active participants or subjects in society. In the final analysis, the praxis of liberation theology is going about the work of social justice.

Enabling the Praxis of Liberation Theology

Praxis finds expression in three distinct, interdependent dimensions: the level of political institutions, human freedom, and faith.

Thomas L. Schubeck, 1993

The idea of facilitating an environment that empowers one to move toward an active subject requires dialogical spaces in which one is an authentic participant where voice is encouraged in the cultivation of democratic spaces. These spaces allow for what Paulo Freire calls *conscientização* (conscientization), an unfolding process that awakens critical awareness, a process that is not static, nor formulaic; rather, conscientization assumes an understanding of our unfinishedness, as we become more aware as knowing subjects of the world in critically examining sociocultural realities.[1] Particularly where unjust forces are at work, the critical examination of reality leads to intentional activism in order to facilitate the transformation or change of that reality. In the end, a more hopeful and critical outlook is mobilized when members of the community are steadily engaged within the three interdependent dimensions of the political, human freedom, and faith, as the Jesuit Thomas L. Schubeck suggests above.[2]

In the light of faith, therefore, the notion of being critically engaged in sociocultural realities requires praxis, suggesting there is no separation between one's faith life and action. Gustavo Gutiérrez would characterize this dynamic as the dialectical interweaving of reflection on the word of God, leading to conversion and the word lived. This transformative activity, Gutiérrez continues, leads individuals from a life of self-centeredness to a life of serving others.[3] In short, as expressed by Harvard Professor of Divinity Emeritus and best-selling author Harvey Cox, "Theology guides action. Action refocuses theology. This continuous process of acting, reflection, then acting again—all in the light of faith—is 'liberation theology.'"[4]

Liberation theology is, of course, about *liberation*, which "expresses the aspirations of oppressed peoples and social classes, emphasizing the conflictual aspect of the economic, social, and political process which puts them at odds with wealthy nations and oppressive classes"[5] To put another way, the notion of liberation suggests that something or someone must be "pushed back" to bring attention to a problem, an unfairness, an injustice. Simultaneously, however, as a historical process, something must be proclaimed in bringing a solution or a way out of that problem or injustice. In other words, the denunciation of any form of dehumanizing activity must be accompanied by the annunciation of the path leading to transformative justice.[6]

And while institutional-structural liberation is critical, Gutiérrez also underscores the importance of internal psychological freedom and the liberation from sin. In the end, sin is the reason for oppression and injustice, impacting values, relationships, and policies.[7] Further making the point, Archbishop Romero recognized, "Suffering will always be. It is a heritage of the first sin and a consequence of the other sins that God permits, even after the redemption. But the redemption converts them into power of salvation when suffering is done in union of faith, hope, and love with the Redeemer's divine suffering and cross."[8] A redemption converted into power suggests that God's grace is not cheap, as the German theologian and vocal dissident of Nazism Dietrich Bonhoeffer (1906–45) put it, further arguing that grace is costly and transformative in which God's gift of freedom liberates us from anxiety, burden, and oppression.[9]

Social Justice as an Expression of Love

Established in the biblical text and informed by the social teachings of the Church, liberation theology is a form of social justice. And social justice in action must necessarily be illuminated by love. That is, fundamental throughout the biblical text is God's love for humanity, first manifested through the creation story in which God saw all that was created as good. In this light, God's love is creative, most particularly culminating in the creation of humankind as partners in love with the divine.[10] And yet despite humanity turning itself against its creator, God's love remained profoundly expressed when the Father sent his only son to be among his people to whom he imparted life-changing teachings, and for whom he ultimately sacrificed his life on the cross. To be sure, the laying down of one's own life for another is the ultimate expression of love.[11]

The depth of God's love, therefore, speaks to the concept of *agape*, a Greek term that expresses the highest form of love, in which no conditions are placed. In other words, *agape* is the type of love that asks for nothing in return; it personifies love in its greatest conceivable form, realizing by its very nature cannot be driven by human effort.[12] Rather, it is a type of love that is eternal, never ceases, and in theological terms is moved by the action of the Holy Spirit (see 1 Cor. 14:1-13).

Indeed, Martin Luther King, Jr. (1929–68), during the 1960s civil rights struggle, often talked about how an *agape* form of love must be the cornerstone of the Civil Rights Movement, exhorting all to rise to the level of "God operating in the human heart," enabling the possibility of what King called the Beloved Community.[13] John Lewis (1940–2020), a tireless civil rights worker and Congressman (D-GA), described this community as "nothing less than the Christian concept of the Kingdom of God on earth."[14]

The notion of building the Kingdom of God on earth is realized to the degree that each one of us accept the warm embrace of God's love and that we demonstrate this love with our neighbor. Regarding the latter, highlighted throughout both the Hebrew and Christian Scriptures, love is demonstrated through action on how we work to set people free from bondage (Exodus story); how we work to further justice (Amos 5); how we work to feed the hungry, take care of the poor, and embrace the stranger (Matthew 25); and how we work to conduct our lives like the "good Samaritan" (Luke 10).

To that end, love is intimately linked to justice. And doing justice is a social endeavor that engages in the realm of equity, equality economics, opportunity, education, health care, employment, race, ethnicity, gender, the environment, and other related issues. The contemporary concept of "social justice" can be traced back to the 1800s by theological and religious circles, evolving into as its central aim to make right the conditions that are unjust and oppressive. Pope Pius XI, in his 1931 encyclical, *Quadragesimo Anno*, was the first to use the term "social justice" in church documents.[15]

Yet, it is worth noting that social justice can be a charged concept, often associated with the political left or progressives by both those in and out of the Church. But the reality—traced down from the teachings of the Hebrew Scriptures to the Christian Scriptures to official church documents—is the Almighty is a God of justice, meaning that "social justice" is not about the right or the left, but rather is something inherently shaped in the image of God.

When all is said and done, social justice work will always be animated with what John Lewis calls "good trouble" in a work that ultimately enables the praxis of liberation theology, which is necessarily informed by love in making a more just, right, and loving world. And for the Catholic teacher in the context of their work, the making of a more just, right, and loving world is one that can be conducted in what I characterize as a critical pedagogy in the light of faith.

A Critical Pedagogy in the Light of Faith

So school is as sacred to me as an Eighth Sacrament.

Lorenzo Milani, 1957

Curriculum and pedagogy are different sides of the same coin. With respect to the former, the contemporary discourse on curriculum has historically been influenced by the work of Ralph Tyler (1902–94), considered the "father" of behavioral objectives, particularly with the international appeal of the publication of his 1949 classic book, *Basic Principles of Curriculum and Instruction.*

With what is known as the Tylerian rationale, it is fundamentally from this text that the categorization of goals, objectives, lesson plans, scope and sequence guides and mastery of learning evaluations emerge. And while these various categorizations have their place, the 1970s began an important era in which the Tylerian rationale was rightly challenged with a reconceptualization of the meaning of curriculum, particularly developed by the curriculum theorist, William Pinar.[1]

With his etymological examination of the term "curriculum," which comes from the Latin infinitive *currere*, implying an action, or a journey, to run the course—meaning that curriculum is not viewed as something tangible—Professor Pinar suggests that the notion of curriculum is an activity, an inward autobiographical journey. Thus, the curriculum is more than the disciplines, the setting of goals and objectives, or the number of prescribed minutes per study of subject matter. Rather, the assumption is that the inner dynamics of a person are inherent, thus, becoming intimately involved in the curriculum, facilitating direction.[2]

In this light, the reconceptualization of the curriculum becomes an inward journey, a human question, linked to the dialectical nature of becoming, concepts related to power, and the favoring or nonfavoring of respective forms of knowledge.[3] Put another way, curriculum work must be historically contextualized, explored, and negotiated, all within the context of conceptions of emancipation.[4]

As to the other side of the coin, pedagogy signifies the art and science of teaching, concretely expressed through the instructional approach taken by the teacher. The suggested difference, therefore, between pedagogy and instruction is that the concept *pedagogy* is driven by a point of view, a belief system, a philosophy of teaching, and *instruction* is the carrying out of that philosophy in action.[5] In that light—mindful of the reconceptualization of the curriculum as a central frame to inform pedagogy—the link to critical pedagogy is organically made.

Critical Pedagogy

The term "critical" is etymologically derived from the Greek root *kriticos* (discerning judgment), suggesting careful evaluation, analysis, or examination of something. The concept of critical pedagogy, therefore, is rooted in the idea of living an examined life relative to the art and science of teaching, obviously connected to the everydayness of practice, the quality of relationships nurtured among students and their families, among faculty and staff, and within the wider community, furthered coupled with existential happenings related to equity, equality, justice, and the political nature of education.

If one were to conduct an examination of the meaning of critical pedagogy, it will become apparent that there are multiple ways to describe it. However, there are central characteristics woven throughout the variety of descriptions. That is, critical pedagogy is theoretically grounded; realizes that there is no such thing as a neutral education; understands that education is political; does not view education from a reductionistic or a deterministic point of view; seeks to comprehend the link between knowledge and power; is contextually attentive; promotes human rights, justice, and democracy; is a process of transformation; is a way of thinking; pays attention to themes related to gender, class, race, and ethnicity and its relationship to forces of oppression and liberation; moves both teacher and student in a horizontal relationship as subjects; challenges the status quo; and is continuously evolving.[6] In short, the thinking of critical pedagogy not only provides a window to understand injustice but also provides what Professor Henry Giroux calls a language of critique and hope.[7]

Critical pedagogy is a call to live an examined life, realizing that a language of critique and hope informs a spirituality that is integral to the thinking of liberation theology, ultimately leading to praxis.[8] The praxis for the Catholic teacher is enabled, as described in Chapter 8, through the dialectical interweaving of faith and practice, a process that recognizes the social justice prism that links critical pedagogy with liberation theology.

Critical pedagogy in the light of faith, therefore, is a way of being, a way of thinking, a way of doing. Moreover, a critical pedagogy in the light of faith seeks to question the structures, policies, economics, and practices that have created the conditions for poverty and marginalization. Finally, a critical pedagogy in the light of faith compels the Catholic teacher to be held accountable, to be engaged, to stay informed, and to make a preferential option for the poor within that sacred space—that "Eight Sacrament"—called schooling.[9]

Poverty must be viewed in terms of its impact on quality of life and a sense of security, safety, and well-being. In this broad sense, poverty is imposed when it works to dehumanize. Discrimination and bigotry because of race, religion, and gender, living in an abusive physical and psychological environment, trapped in a home setting that is a revolving door of drug and alcohol abuse, ensnared or diseased by addictions or psychological destructive behavior, dealing with the constant pangs of food depravation, and the daily struggle to economically make it— these are all dehumanizing realities. In the end, as articulated by Father Henri Nouwen (1932–96), "Poverty creates marginal people, people who are separated from that whole network of ideas, services, facilities and opportunities that support human beings in times of crisis."[10] It is for these—students and their families who are on the margins—that the Catholic teacher must make a preferential option.[11]

Making a Pedagogical Choice for a Preferential Option for the Poor

The task of making a preferential option for the poor requires an intentional pedagogical choice. This choice necessitates awareness, an awareness that the poor and marginalized have historically been labeled and routinely objectified with such terms, among other labels, as the "urban underclass," the "deprived," the "disadvantaged," the "underprivileged," the "homeless," "street people," the "underemployed," "welfare queens," the "at-risk," the "underachievers," "those people," and the "have-nots."[12] Particularly with respect to schooling, the danger of these labels blind us "to the complex lives lived out in the classroom."[13] In the final analysis, whether it objectifies, binds, or excludes, it is never a good thing to be poor;[14] the likely negative impact for school-aged students who live in poverty is undeniable in comparison to their non-poor peers.

That is, among other negative consequences, children who live in poverty are more likely to experience low birth weight, food insecurity (i.e., not having enough to eat, poor diet, parents' inability to consistently purchase adequate, nutritious food), chronic health ailments such as asthma and anemia; to live in substandard housing; to be raised by parents/caregivers with minimal years of formal education; to live in households with little cognitive stimulation, negatively impacting cognitive and academic success; to manifest inappropriate behavior, disobedience, impulsiveness, emotional issues, and poor peer interaction; to be exposed to parental substance abuse, violent crime, environmental toxins, and minimal quality child care services; to live in substandard, unsafe neighborhoods; to be subjected to frequent moves, family structure changes; and to remain poor as an adult.[15]

Given the impact poverty can have on the affected population, the task of making a preferential option thus also recognizes that education is primarily about entering into relationships with students and their families, allowing for the possibilities to understand the complex lives lived out in the classroom.[16] Indeed, the cultivating of meaningful relationships is integral in fostering an authentic teaching and learning schooling environment. And compassion is imperative within that environment.

Linked to the qualities of empathy and care, the term "compassion" comes from the Latin *compati*, meaning to be conscious and aware of another's difficulty and distress while simultaneously seeking out possible solutions and alternatives to alleviate anxiety and troubles. That is, the Catholic teacher must not only demonstrate a competency in their pedagogical practice and be intimately aware of their students' various dilemmas and struggles but also continuously aim for constructive and practical strategies and solutions, leading to reassurance and affirmation for each individual student.

To be sure, the Catholic teacher (all teachers) must make every attempt to meet the needs of *all* students enrolled in class, yet at the same time is aware of what it means to make a preferential option. Stated another way, making a preferential option does not come at the expense of excluding or neglecting the non-poor; rather, it is a particular attentiveness to matters of equity for the poor. Equity is about working toward leveling the playing field, about fairness, about justice.

There is a popular image that vividly portrays the notion of equity with three adolescents standing to watch a sporting event from behind a wooden fence. The first adolescent can see the event perfectly well because he is tall enough to see over the fence. The second one stands on her tip-toes, barely viewing the event over the fence. And the third one is not able to see over the fence because he is not tall enough. The solution for the adolescent on her tip-toes is to provide a crate for her to stand on so she can comfortably view the event; for the adolescent who is not able to see at all, a taller crate is provided so that he can comfortably stand and see; and, for the one who is comfortably viewing the event, no crate is necessary. Albeit a rudimentary image, it concretely illustrates the point: with all three young people now comfortably viewing the event, a sense of equity has been launched.

From a Micro Level

To that end, from a micro level, within a classroom setting and knowing the potential impact the effect poverty can have on school-aged youth, making a preferential option may require the teacher to take extra time with a student to make sure he or she is grasping the material, and if necessary may seek to help before and/or after school, even looking to provide with extra tutoring by peers or other adults. Moreover, the teacher remains attentive that an affected student has the proper nourishment, the appropriate school supplies, and suitable clothing. Finally, the teacher is attentive to the voice of parents and caregivers, keeping them regularly informed regarding the schooling status of their children, and, if need be, ready to offer suggestions regarding social, civic, or religious agencies that may provide assistance in whatever needed capacity.

Assuredly, the teacher must still look to challenge a respective student to a high standard of excellence, but in such a way that is tempered with making connections to a student's background knowledge and experiences, and working within the student's zone of proximal development.[17] This process involves a pedagogical approach rooted in love, guided by hope, and laced with patience, consistency, and persistence, recognizing the importance of establishing dialogical spaces whereby students are empowered as willing participants, as subjects, within an environment that values age-appropriate and culturally relevant practices.[18]

From a Macro Level

From a macro level, the Catholic teacher must be politically and socially aware, particularly when it comes to policies and practices that positively or negatively impact the common good. According to the Catechism of the Catholic Church, the common good—with the state playing a central role to defend and promote—is featured through respecting individual persons, building the social well-being and development of the group, and cultivating peace and justice.[19]

In other words, respecting the dignity of every human being in terms of needs, services, and opportunities must work in such a way that it simultaneously benefits the individual and builds the entire community. Indeed, as the *Compendium of the Social Doctrine of the Church* puts it, the common good suggests that "*The human person cannot find fulfilment in himself, that is, apart from the fact that he exists 'with' others and 'for' others*" (author's emphasis).[20]

In that light, consider a neoliberal philosophy that has had a significant influence on the economic, social, and education trajectory worldwide. Linked to globalization, neoliberalism is propelled by a practice driven by competition, individualism, the market, privatization, and profit. In and of themselves, there is nothing wrong with the notion of competition, intricacies of the market, the place of individualism, private practice, and the workings of profit, each of which and collectively comes with great responsibility and accountability. Neoliberalism, however, has no interest in regulation, collaboration, cooperation, and the good of the group, looking to dismantle the public square, public spaces, public education. And what gets lost—when deregulation, unrestricted competition, and unbridled profiteering acts as the final arbiter—is the common good.[21]

It is no coincidence when there is a push that looks to weaken government social programs or to minimize breakfast and school lunch initiatives or to incessantly test students, or to defund public parks, libraries, public K–12 education, or public university systems. It is no coincidence to spread a storyline that blames the poor for the economic and social conditions they find themselves.[22] Neoliberalism is an economic and social system that cultivates—ironically—a regulation about how people ought to act. And if they do not act a certain way, as dictated by that viewpoint, then the problem is them and not the viewpoint that created the conditions of their problem, that is, poverty.

In other words, for neoliberal thought to function, it has to have a scapegoat to advance its agenda.

It is an agenda in which economic, social, and schooling realities have become sport in deciding who the "winners" and "losers" are; it is the poor and marginalized who suffer the greatest in this warped system. In the denunciation of such a system, what must be announced is a system that looks to collaborate in building up the entire community, the common good—which is linked to solidarity.

Solidarity

Marcus Rashford is star professional footballer (or soccer player) who plays both for Manchester in the Premier League and England's national team. As much as he has stamped his international mark as an athlete, he has done the same as an advocate for the plight of the poor in the UK.

In 2020, when the government threatened to end the voucher meal program for disenfranchised families during the summer of the Covid-19 crisis, Rashford—with a groundswell of public support— became a powerful voice in compelling the then Prime Minister Boris Johnson to pivot with continuance of the program. Still later that same year, when once again the government threatened to discontinue the meal program during the holidays, Rashford remained steadfast with his insistence of not letting that happen, again affecting the government to change course to continue on with the food initiative.[23]

Since around 2010 the UK has witnessed cuts in spending for public services, such as in food distribution programs, obviously exacerbating food insecurity among the poor.[24] Hence, the necessity of voices, such as Rashford's, who dealt with food insecurity as a child: "My mum worked full-time, earning the minimum wage, to make sure we always had a good evening meal on the table, but it was not enough … The system was not built for families like mine to succeed, regardless of how hard my mum worked."[25]

Clearly, when systems are not properly in place in order to cultivate the common good, real people are affected no matter how hard they are trying to make it. Rashford experientially understands that—a young man beyond his years with the presence of a personalist disposition that grounds the center of his gravity, vowing, "This is not politics, this is humanity. These children matter. These children are the future of this country. They are not just another statistic. And for as long as they don't have a voice, they will have mine."[26]

Not only does Rashford lend his voice but he also visits and spends time forming relationships with those who struggle with poverty. Indeed, with his words and actions, while Rashford courageously calls out systems at work to dehumanize, he is committed to the cause of the humanization of humanity with a vision of a better world in which all can partake. To state it differently, Rashford demonstrates what it means to be in solidarity with the poor.

In his Encyclical, *Sollicitudo Rei Socialis* (*The Social Concerns of the Church*), Pope John Paul II made the point that solidarity is not a vague compassion for the misfortunates of peoples near and far. Rather, "it [solidarity] is a firm and persevering determination to commit oneself to the common good; that is to say to the good of all and of each individual, because we are all really responsible for all."[27]

For Catholic teachers, in their realization that curriculum is the other side of the same coin as pedagogy, making the connection to critical pedagogy and its link to liberation theology and the social teachings of the Church, and in particular making a preferential option for the poor and recognizing the importance of cultivating the common good in a spirit of solidarity—it ought to be clear why a critical pedagogy in the light of faith has its necessary place.

This, therefore, requires the Catholic teacher to understand that taking a position of neutrality is not an option, as that is only giving a nod to the status quo; rather, what is required by the Catholic teacher is to be spiritually and theologically grounded and socially, politically, and educationally informed on what establishes their point of view, while realizing the light of hope that guides them (see 1 Pet. 3:15).

Marcus Rashford is more than a professional athlete. He is a humanitarian. In the same way, Catholic teachers are more than about "reading, writing, and arithmetic." Their work requires them to be involved in the varied forces that impact the lives of their students both in and out of the school building. And where those forces negatively impact the schooling experience through an assessment system that does not work or marginalizes, or breakfast and lunch programs that are insufficient, or after-school programs that are lacking, or the labeling of students in pigeon-hole categories, or where there is a dearth of resources and extra-curricular opportunities, or inadequate health services, the Catholic teacher must be a voice, an activist voice of solidarity.

Indeed, that voice of solidarity recognizes that as a Catholic teacher, taking a position is a necessary critical responsibility, which furthermore—as a participant in life—extends beyond the school building, particularly as it relates to highly charged political and social issues that have stung our twenty-first-century global community, a theme that will be explored in Section III of this book.

Section III

Know Your Positionality: Confronting a Pandemic, Gun Control, Right to Life, and Climate Change

The Courage to Take a Position

Positionality asserts that knowledge is dependent upon a complex web of cultural values, beliefs, experiences, and social positions. The ability to situate oneself as knower in relationship to that which is known is widely acknowledged as fundamental to understanding the political, social, and historical dimensions of knowledge. Positionality is a foundation of this examination.

Sensoy & DiAngelo, 2017

There is an assignment I do in one of my graduate classes in which I ask students, all of whom typically live in different geographic regions of the country (and some in other parts of the world), to write a letter to the editor for their local newspaper. The letter can be one in which the student asserts a particular position about any number of political, social, cultural, religious, or education themes, or it can be written as a response to a newspaper article or commentary on any of those themes. Upon hearing the expectations for the assignment, it is not uncommon that several students in the class are a bit nervous and even resistant to the project. They fear that by taking a public position in the newspaper, they will open themselves to pushback, even if they might also receive affirmation.

We then discuss why remaining "neutral" or silent on any number of issues simply contributes to the status quo. In other words, and in particular for the Catholic teacher, as Fr. Richard Rohr, insightfully puts it, "*There is no such thing as a nonpolitical Christianity.* To refuse to critique the system or the status quo is to fully support it—which is a political act well disguised" (author's emphasis).[1] It takes a certain amount of courage to speak up, to speak out, through any number of media, such as the newspaper.

In taking a position, one must know, as James A. Banks, the "father" of multicultural education, suggests, "the important difference between opinion and informed knowledge."[2] To be sure, with respect to the latter, educators must critically take the initiative to be informed by quality and varied informational sources, with a reflective disposition and considering the complexities inherent in the social, political, cultural, and religious aspects of life. And for the Catholic educator, all of this must be grounded through the lens of faith, through a spirit of hope, gentleness, reverence, and a clear conscience.[3]

Accordingly, the vocation of the Catholic teacher extends beyond the confines of a school building, obliging one to be thoughtfully engaged in any number of sometimes charged political, social, and cultural matters, which in some form will always intersect with education. While multiple themes can be discussed, in the interest of space I limit the focus to four particularly highly charged issues: Covid-19 pandemic, gun control, the right to life, and climate change. And whether you agree or not with my point of view, even in regard to other discussed themes in this book, I hope the following chapter discussions will serve as a catalyst to heightened reflection and further crystalize your own respective positionality, foundational to examination.[4]

Covid-19 and a Peculiar Toxic Discourse

Lord, make me an instrument of your peace.

St. Francis of Assisi (1181/82–1226)

It was in December 2019 when the World Health Organization (WHO) took notice about a coronavirus emerging out of Wuhan, China. In the collective coronaviruses (CoVs) trigger severe acute respiratory syndrome (SARS), as was in the case of the 2003 outbreak of SARS-CoV, leading to the designation of this new virus as SARS-CoV-2, now known as Covid-19. In terms of the latter, "Co" signifies corona (crown), "vi" signifies virus, and "d" signifies disease, and "19" means 2019.[1] Since Covid-19 emerged and as of this writing, over 500 million confirmed cases have been reported from around the globe, with many people dealing with long-term effects, and with over six million dying from the disease worldwide.[2]

Despite years of ample warnings, the United States, indeed the world, was underprepared for this type of virus.[3] Yet through the nonstop, valiant efforts of the medical and scientific community, as we were moving into spring 2021, a hopeful outlook permeated the air, paving a path through the other side of the pandemic with a steady stream of people getting vaccinated in the United States, Great Britain, Israel, and other countries.

This was just the beginning, as efforts were in place to distribute the vaccine to other countries; however, the process has been slow. That spring, it was reasonably thought, that by the start of the 2021–2 academic school year in the United States, we would be back to some kind of normalization. The assumption was that people would continue to do their part by getting vaccinated and/or masking/social distancing when necessary. But a disease of toxicity was brewing beneath that hopeful assumption.

From the get-go, the politics of Covid-19 were evident, but it progressively took a more vitriolic path. From the virus's origins, with the anti-Asian racialized hostility that ensued, to how it spread, to the polemics of mandates, masking, and vaccinating, to the undermining of the scientific and medical community, to the economic, social, and schooling impact—the political climate seemed to come to a head during summer 2021, shattering the hope that seemed within our reach. In short, the dark side of politics eclipsed the light of public safety. And, of course, educators in particular have been entangled in the fray of this pandemic storm, which has required them to be informed and demanded they take a position. As a result, the politics of the virus became a social justice issue.

At the rollout of the vaccine in January 2021, Pope Francis viewed getting vaccinated as a moral obligation, not only for oneself but also for the lives of others in whom we encounter.[4] To be clear, however, the Pope was obviously aware that there are particular medical reasons that would prevent some people from receiving the vaccination.[5] Later, in August 2021, speaking to the world community, but particularly addressing the resistance of the vaccine in the United States, the Pope declared that getting the vaccine was an "an act of love," further emphasizing that the "Vaccination is a simple but profound way of promoting the common good and caring for each other, especially the most vulnerable."[6]

Even with the medical community overwhelmingly endorsing the effectiveness and safety of the vaccination and the efficacy of social distancing and mask-wearing (particularly a heightened necessity for the unvaccinated), alongside the pleas of the Pope and many other high-profile leaders, large portions of the US population, at times with a warped sense of individual liberties, had mockingly tuned out.

Thus, when political philosopher Michael Sandel asserts that the United States was "morally unprepared" to deal with the pandemic, he is right. He suggests that the notion of individualism has blinded many to value solidarity and the common good that the Pope speaks of.[7] And that blindness has cost us. During the early months of 2022, as the Delta and Omicron variants were in full force, many more people had unnecessarily perished or had gotten quite sick.

Looking toward the Other Side of the Pandemic?

Of course, not every Covid-19-related death or illness is avoidable. Yet the preventable measures enunciated by the medical community and the rapid production of a safe vaccine have saved lives and averted serious illness, a phenomenon nothing short of heroic. This is not even a question. And, as of this writing, with mask mandates being lifted in many parts of the world, with fewer travel restrictions, with folks going about their business in a more normal fashion—shopping, eating out, and attending crowded sporting and entertainment events—it appears we are looking toward the other side of the pandemic.

It would be foolhardy to think we are totally out of the woods, as the emergence of other variants (and subvariants) is expected, with some more lethal than others, and some more contagious than others. Time will only tell how all this will play out, but without question, health officials strongly urge caution moving forward. Of course, humankind has always been challenged with the presence of viruses; it is a natural coexistence. But what has compounded the latter during the Covid-19 crisis is a particular, even peculiar, vitriolic attack on the medical and science community. The reason for these threats is varied, such as those who believe that the virus is a hoax or was intentionally created to harm, or that the vaccines are unsafe.[8]

Harassment, personal attacks, and threats are endured by those who have appeared on any number of media outlets, whether it be in the United States, Germany, the United Kingdom, Brazil, Australia, or other parts of the world. For example, in my home state of South Carolina, infectious disease physician Dr. Krutika Kuppalli, at the

Medical University of South Carolina in Charleston (now with WHO in Geneva, Switzerland), had to withstand hostile emails and phone calls as a consequence of her high-profile media appearances discussing Covid-19, coupled with her testifying before a US congressional committee on how elections can be conducted safely in the midst of a pandemic. And because there were threats on her life, the police suggested that Kuppalli purchase a gun to protect herself. A civil society? I think not; yet, this is where we are, and particularly during the pandemic, Kuppalli's experience, among researchers and public health officials, is disturbingly common.[9]

Perhaps the greatest variant to have emerged from the Covid-19 crisis is the toxic nature of discourse that works to dehumanize, to undermine truth, reason, logic, and the public good. It is a discourse bent on tribalism as opposed to harmonization; a discourse that finds a warped pleasure in attacking as opposed to reaching toward common-ground sensibilities; a discourse that is based on arrogant pride as opposed to a spirit of humility that looks to dialogically reason together; and a discourse that leads to violence, even death, as opposed to one that fosters life and community.

Clearly, as we look into the horizon, much work needs to be done if we have any hope to cooperatively and collaboratively work together when it comes to confronting a pandemic or any other national or global crises. Indeed, as Jesus cautions, "And no town or house divided against itself will stand."[10] And, so, perhaps the greatest of that work is to look in the mirror and ask, "What I am doing to build, to understand, to extend a hand, to reach across?" It seems only appropriate to end this chapter with the prayer that is attributed to St. Francis of Assisi:

> Lord, make me an instrument of your peace.
> Where there is hatred let me sow love;
> Where there is injury, pardon;
> Where there is doubt, faith;
> Where there is despair, hope;
> Where there is darkness, light;
> Where there is sadness, joy.

O Divine Master, grant that I may not so much seek
To be consoled as to console;
To be understood as to understand;
To be loved as to love.
For it is in giving that we receive;
It is in pardoning that we are pardoned;
And it is in dying that we are born to eternal life.[11]

God, Guns, and Country

When are we going to do something?

Steve Kerr, 2022

When I was a child growing up in the Tuscany area of Italy, my family lived directly across the street from a stretch of woods, which I often explored. I recall during certain times of the year in the very early mornings, I would be awakened by interval sounds of "pow, pow, pow." As each of my siblings would then arise, we would mutter, "The hunters are out." That would certainly not be a time to be exploring the woods. In our area, the prey of choice were pheasants. And after the hunt, it was not uncommon to see hunters walking home, with rifles slung over one shoulder, with their catch in tow, stringed up on the other shoulder. The hunting season in Italy can go anywhere from September to February, not only for birds but also for wild boar, deer, and rabbits.

While my parents did not hunt, nor did we have any type of firearms around the house, I thought nothing of the hunters walking home strapped with rifles; it was simply a part of the fabric of my upbringing. Moreover, I did not have any further reflections regarding gun ownership and was not aware of any news reports regarding what we now call mass shootings. Indeed, at that time (1960s–1970s) indiscriminate shootings were quite rare and virtually unheard of in a school setting. While there are varied definitions in the literature regarding what constitutes a mass shooting, according to the Gun Violence Archive, it is one in which at least four victims are shot, either killed or injured (not including the shooter who may have been shot or killed).[1] Of course, the idea of hunting is obviously a separate and distinctly different than a conversation on mass shootings.

In fact, there is a certain gun culture in Italy, backed by a strong political lobby on behalf of hunters. Yet, mass shootings in Italy are essentially non-existent, in large measure because of strict laws regarding gun ownership and the kinds of arms that are allowed under the law.[2] Unlike the United States, Italy does not have constitutional language that provides for arms ownership as in the Second Amendment.

The Advent of the Second Amendment

The mindset that shaped the Second Amendment in the US Constitution goes back to ancient Rome and Florence with the espousal of the citizen soldier. While the concept of a militia can be traced back to ancient Macedonia, its English origins were launched in the sixteenth century under the reign of Queen Elizabeth I, during which a national militia was instituted. Albeit not successful under the Queen's rule, the idea of the possibilities of a militia (or citizen soldier) flourished, particularly demonstrated in colonial America, the American Revolution, the War of 1812, and the American Civil War.[3]

In short, a militia is comprised of the citizenry to defend the community or homeland on as a needed basis. The formation of an armed part-time citizenry militia was favored because of a prevailing mistrust of a professional or standing military who at its whim could threaten freedom, the free state. Thus, the advent of the Second Amendment, stating, "A well regulated Militia, being necessary to the security of a free State, the right of the people to keep and bear Arms, shall not be infringed."[4]

It has been well over 200 years since the adoption of the Second Amendment, and the idea of a standing military is an embraced norm, often validated with common patriotic parlance to thank those who are serving in the armed services and honor veterans who have served. Over the last two centuries, debate has been continuous regarding the interpretation of the Second Amendment.[5] That is, does the Amendment allow for private citizens to possess arms, or was this possession only to be as a collective right as through a militia unit (contemporarily the National Guard and State Defense Forces)?

The 2008 Supreme Court landmark case *District of Columbia v. Heller* finally settled that question, allowing the right for individuals to bear arms for self-protection (self-defense), furthered confirmed in the controversial 2010 *McDonald v. City of Chicago* case, which through the Fourteenth Amendment due process clause, extended federal law to state and local laws.[6] In the end, whether one agrees or not with the interpretation of the Second Amendment relative to present-day America, US citizens have the right to bear arms, validating a gun culture in the United States.

God, Guns, and Country

One can easily go a step further, however, arguing that that there is a distinctly American religious fervor when it comes to this gun culture, especially summed up with any number of related common bumper stickers, such as "God, Guns, and Country." The conflating of weaponry with God and further linked to patriotism is a curious zealous brand that generally has no concern with the number of firearms one ought to own, the type of weapons one possesses, and minimal requirements for gun ownership. For example, in 2021 Texas added to their already lax gun ownership requirements by legislatively allowing citizens to carry a handgun without a license.

Citizens in the United States own approximately 120.5 guns for every 100 persons, in contrast to Italy, where citizens own approximately 14.4 guns for every 100 persons. And in Italy, compared to the United States, there are strict restrictions regarding the kinds of firearms one can own and who can own (compare endnote 2 with 7).[7] On the whole, compared to all other countries, US civilians own more guns per capita than civilians in any other country in the world. And this ownership has manifested itself in all sorts of disturbing ways, such as a high rate of suicides, homicides, and mass shootings deaths (not to mention the wounded), all of which have become a distinctive American phenomenon.[8]

With respect to this phenomenon, John R. Allen, president of the Brookings Institution and retired US Marine Corps four-star general and former commander of the NATO International Security Assistance Force (ISAF) and U.S. Forces in Afghanistan, explains it this way: "Gun violence in America has become a national security emergency."[9] Schools were once thought as being a safe haven for school-aged youth, but that reality has been shattered with over 50 percent of teenagers worried about the possibility of a school shooting at their respective schools. Indeed, their parents share their concern, as well.[10]

In addition, since the 1999 Columbine School massacre, the anxiety level of teachers persists regarding the possibility of school shootings and other forms of violence on the school campus.[11] And while the proliferation of gun violence in the United States is now considered a very real health concern, even a national epidemic, the response to this proliferation from the National Rifle Association (NRA), the powerful gun lobby group in the United States, is "The only thing that stops a bad guy with a gun, is a good guy with a gun."[12] In other words, having more guns at our disposal is the solution to this real and present danger. And it is that one response, that mindset, which has contributed to a culture of violence in the United States.

Clinical psychologist Ana Nogles makes the point that a culture of violence views weaponry as a symbol of power. The firearm industry is a multi-billion-dollar enterprise, and the United States has a history of violence since its founding. Moreover, as Nogles asserts, there is a tendency to glamorize violence through a variety of social media that can work to desensitize minds, especially those of young people, and even legitimize violence as a conflict resolution, ultimately making this issue a personal, social, and political problem.[13] The idea of stopping a bad guy with a gun with a good guy with a gun is not only a simplistic trivialization of a disturbing American problem but is also unrealistic; rather, the reality is that gun independence, increased gun ownership, and a rise in open-carry laws have led to more violence, homicide rates, and road rage.[14]

Common-Sense Measures

While there is no one single solution to mitigate America's gun problem, the United States Conference of Catholic Bishops (USCCB) support what is characterized as common-sense measures, worthwhile to note here:

- A total ban on assault weapons, which the USCCB supported when the ban passed in 1994 and when Congress failed to renew it in 2004;
- Measures that control the sale and use of firearms, such as universal background checks for all gun purchases;
- Limitations on civilian access to high-capacity weapons and ammunition magazines;
- A federal law to criminalize gun trafficking;
- Improved access to and increased resources for mental health care and earlier interventions;
- Regulations and limitations on the purchasing of handguns;
- Measures that make guns safer, such as locks that prevent children and anyone other than the owner from using the gun without permission and supervision; and
- An honest assessment of the toll of violent images and experiences which inundate people, particularly our youth.[15]

In addition to the above, there is strong advocacy from the USCCB regarding the banning of "bump stocks" (allowing a rifle to rapidly fire over and over) and Extreme Risk Protection Orders (ERPOs or "red flag laws"), which is a temporary removal of firearms from someone who may be a threat to oneself or others. The USCCB also advocates education, discussions, and community involvement that fosters peacebuilding through restorative justice initiatives.[16]

Finally, the idea of open carry should be more restrictively regulated—better yet, prohibited—as advocated by Everytown for Gun Safety, one of the largest gun violence prevention organizations in the

United States.[17] As demonstrated in other countries, as in the case of Italy, and in some pockets of the United States, these aforementioned common-sense measures have proven to reduce the perpetration of gun violence. The Giffords Law Center to Prevent Gun Violence, while obviously recognizing the public health crisis that is gun violence, the center emphasizes in an encouraging, resolute way, "Solutions exist [e.g., USCCB, Everytown for Gun Safety, Giffords Law Center to Prevent Gun Violence proposals], but we need leaders with the courage to act." May we all possess the courage to act and join in these sensibilities.[18] Yet.

Postscript

Only a few short days after submitting a completed draft of this manuscript to my editor, three mass shootings occurred within a ten-day period in May 2022: Uvalde, Texas, at Robb Elementary School (May 24, 21 killed, nineteen children and two teachers); Laguna Woods, California, at Irvine Taiwanese Presbyterian Church (May 15, 1 killed, five injured); Buffalo, New York, at a Topps Supermarket (May 14, ten killed, three injured). As if that were not bad enough, from January through May 2022 there were 214 mass shootings in the United States, not even the half-way through the year![19] Sadly, tragically, terribly, by the time you read this book, more shootings, mayhem, death, and injury will litter the American landscape.

So, when former NBA player and current NBA coach Steve Kerr passionately exclaimed right after the Uvalde, Texas, massacre, "When are we going to do something?" he voiced the cry of the majority of Americans, indeed the world![20] In a powerful piece, the *Miami Herald*'s Editorial Board writes,

> Here we are again, counting the bodies of dead kids … Why can't we stop this very American form of slaughter? But here we are. More than that, here we are again. A little more than four years after the Parkland school shooting in Florida. Six years since the Pulse nightclub shooting. A decade after Sandy Hook Elementary. Days after

the Buffalo, New York, supermarket killings. And on and on, on, on. Will things change? Do we just have to live with this obscenity in our midst? Can we? It is tempting to let despair take over, to hide from the pain convulsing our country as we try to come to terms with yet another male gunman arming himself with weapons of war, buying far too many rounds of ammunition and murdering innocents … We act like there's nothing we can do. But there are things we can do.[21]

Just three days after the killings of the innocents at Robb Elementary School, the NRA met for its annual conference in Houston, Texas, less than 300 miles from Uvalde. And the thematic mantra at the conference was the same—"The only thing that stops a bad guy with a gun, is a good guy with a gun"—coupled with pushing the idea of arming teachers with weaponry and securing schools with armed guards. According to this line of thinking, we shouldn't even consider the common-sense proposals asserted by the USCCB, Everytown for Gun Safety, and Giffords Law Center to Prevent Gun Violence proposals; the solution is to turn our schools into battle forts.

It is tempting to let despair take over, but indeed we cannot. Hope must be kept alive, faith must remain in tack, and love must continue to reign in our hearts, all of which must resolutely propel our social and political activism to do the things we can do to promote the sensibilities through which a culture of life can be built.

13

Preserving the Sacredness of Life

If there is a child that you don't want or can't feed or educate, give that child to me. I will not refuse any child. I will give a home, or find loving parents for him or for her.

Mother Teresa, 1994

Some years ago, I heard what has now become an unforgettable gentle knock on my apartment door. I answered, and there stood my neighbor, a young woman, who I will call Molly. With worry written on her face, she asked to speak to me and straightaway uttered that she had scheduled an abortion for the very next day. "What do you think; what should I do?" she asked. While Molly had a general idea that my faith was important to me, we had only superficially spoken a few times prior to this encounter; I barely knew her.

So, I was rather surprised that she had asked to speak to me about a matter so personal. She explained that she had gotten pregnant in a casual encounter, with no plans to stay with the man, and was not in a financial or emotional position to raise a child. At first glance, I was not quite sure how to respond to something quite this heavy, yet I realized that my neighbor was conflicted and, for reasons only known to her, had reached out to me.

What a miraculous moment in the darkness and warmth of a woman's body that the light of conception is made. Rooted in the biblical text and reinforced with subsequent ecclesial documents, the Catholic Church is clear about when life begins and unambiguous about its position on abortion.[1] In some sense, once conception occurs, the newly created genetic structure has nothing to do with the man or woman who conducted the production; it now has everything to do with the creation of a brand-new unique life.[2] But, of course, it also has everything to do with the woman and man, naturally, especially the woman. Within as early as five and a half to six weeks a fetal heartbeat can be detected in the developing embryo. And at the six-and-a-half- to seven-week mark a heartbeat can be better evaluated. A spring of new life has come to visit, with a "leap in the womb."[3]

Pondering how to best respond to Molly now sitting nervously in my living room, I was familiar with the teachings of the Church. These teachings, however, have a long history, an uneven history in which an intersected discourse about morality, contraception, ethics, animation, ensoulment, abortion, homicide, penance, punishment, forgiveness, religion, theology, and politics have collided into a heated polemic that has been ongoing throughout the ages, even before the time of Christ.

A Bit of History

Since the dawn of the Christian Church, the question was not so much whether the Church viewed abortion as a moral wrong, an affront to God; it always has. Rather, the question—particularly for the early Church—was when did the embryo become human or a being and when did ensoulment (possess a soul) occur? For these questions, the early Church looked to their Jewish brethren—to whom Pope John Paul II called our "beloved brothers, in a certain way, one could say our older brothers" (see Chapter 2)—and looked to the available science, that which was particularly propagated by Aristotle.

Aristotle suggested that forty days after conception a male fetus was formed, and after ninety days a female. Thus, the idea of an "unformed" and "formed" fetus entered the lexicon, meaning the latter constituted animation, quickening, or ensoulment of the fetus as opposed to delayed animation or ensoulment for the former. While abortion was generally an accepted practice in ancient Greece, Aristotle seemingly argues that once the fetus is "formed" and the idea of ensoulment is taking place, abortion then becomes unacceptable.[4]

For the Jews, the act of deliberate killing violates the Ten Commandments, realizing the significance of the distinct sanctity of life that is born out of the image of God (*imago Dei*) as it states in Genesis. The embryo is viewed as mere fluid until the fortieth day, at that point moving into a state of potential life, thus making the fetus an organic part of the mother and not a separate being until birth.[5]

To be sure, however, it is this potential of life that possesses obvious inherent sacred, developmental value, meaning that abortion "diminishes God's image."[6] And while there are various branches or streams of Judaism (e.g., Reform, Conservative, Orthodox, secular), there is not a monolithic Jewish point of view when it comes to abortion, though it is overall seen as a moral wrong, except to save the mother's life and in other extenuating circumstances.[7]

It was in this collective light that informed Augustine, and later Thomas Aquinas and others who continued to wonder at what point did ensoulment occur and at what juncture was abortion considered a homicide. While the biblical text and early Church writings (e.g., Didache, Epistle of Barnabas, and the Apocalypse of Peter) had already established that abortion was a sinful act, regardless of the status of the fetus, a demarcation was made regarding the canonical penalties levied relative to when an abortion was conducted. These penalties and absolvent processes have a complicated history and were different for an aborted fetus prior to the forty-day mark than for those after that period, naturally more stringent for the latter than the former.[8]

Fast forward into the seventeenth century: with the benefit of scientific progress within the ongoing process of the Church grappling with the moral, ethical, and spiritual questions regarding the development and formation of the fetus, the Church ultimately concluded that an Aristotelian-influenced position was no longer viable. Thus, in 1869 with the release of *Apostolicae Sedis* by Pope Pius IX, the distinction between a "formed" (animated) and "unformed" (unanimated) fetus was removed from canon law. Moreover, biological breakthroughs determined that at fertilization, with the formation of a zygote, chromosomal determination is made that determines the sex of the being, meaning the establishment of a unique life has been put into motion. In that light, the Church determined that life begins at the point of conception.[9]

Trained as a physician, popular, award-winning novelist and Catholic convert, Walker Percy sums up the point:

> Any doctor can tell you that an unborn child is fully human. There is no difference between a child five minutes before birth and five minutes after birth. What about a month before birth? Same. How about eight months? How about one day after conception? Sure. It's a separate organism. Any doctor will tell you that it's all standard biology: the fetus is a separate genetic structure, a separate immune system ... A separate creature.[10]

Compassion, Love, and Hope

It was this mindset that shaped my thinking as I was conversing with Molly. Yet, my thought process in the course of our conversation was not to come across as judgmental or self-righteous; rather, my hope was that I exerted compassion, love, and hope. As she intently listened regarding my response on what she should do, I shared with her that there were other options than to seek an abortion and that I would assist her in any way possible.[11]

"But what will God think of me if I do this?" she questioned. As I understand the teachings of the Church and the biblical text, I gently responded that God would not be happy, would be gravely disappointed. But God's love for you would not change; God's love is everlasting. Of course, I continued, "There are emotional, psychological, physiological, and spiritual ramifications as a result of an abortion." But, again, as I shared with her, "That does not mean that God won't heal, restore, and forgive, if one earnestly seeks it out."

It took courage for Molly to knock on my door, and I suppose my approach in our exchange was one that looked to persuade, in the light of love and truth, as opposed to coerce in a spirit of condemnation. One could say I was lightly coming from a position of virtue ethics, which is a point of view that looks to appeal to the moral character of an individual in order to facilitate a process in which one makes good and right choices when it comes to ethical and even spiritual dilemmas. Stephen L. Carter, professor of law at Yale and former clerk to US Supreme Court Justice Thurgood Marshall, states, "When women seek abortions, there are *reasons* that they do" (author emphasis).[12] And whatever those reasons may be, whether one agrees or understands them or not, those reasons are a calling out.

In other words, as Carter continues, abortion is symptomatic of a greater problem, which is all at once intertwined with the ethical, moral, social, racial, biological, economical, psychological, emotional, spiritual, legal, and political. Within that intertwining sphere, the ultimate societal question can be tailored down to whether our value system looks toward building what Pope John Paul II calls a culture of death or a culture of life.[13] And if it is to be the latter, then, along with the support of the faith and civic community, private, state, and federal entities must work to sustain that culture of life to promote respectful minimal wages as opposed to balk at such possibilities: to ensure access to health care, child care, paid paternal leave, and other safety nets as opposed to fiscal cuts, difficulties to access, and minimal opportunities.

Being pro-life, therefore, suggests the passionate voice for the personhood of the fetus must be the same voice that advocates for access, opportunity, equality, and equity; the same voice for the poor, the refugee, the asylum seeker, the marginalized, the disabled, and the elderly; and the same voice that denounces racism, homophobia, and hatred of any kind, all of which are linked to the greater problem. In short, being pro-life is a way of life from the "womb-to-the-tomb" in the effort toward building the humanization of humanity.

As Molly and I were concluding our conversation, my mind flooded with the internal acknowledgment that while a woman's body is obviously her own for choices to make, this did not in any way diminish the certain reverence I had for the personhood in her womb.[14] And this personhood and Molly are one, yet separate entities, connected to the common good. And the common good is always about preserving life for all. And preserving life is about justice in which the moral test is about how the most vulnerable members of a society are faring, which must include those in the womb.

Perhaps I could have been more forceful or persuasive; perhaps the idea of abortion has been normalized, providing a rationalized desensitized shield; perhaps we have become so absorbingly individualistic that "I alone will be my reference point";[15] perhaps fear in all its forms linked to family, social, and economic realities took over—Molly had her baby aborted. Who knows what that child may have become and what the preciousness of that soul would have brought to Molly's life, to her community, to the world. God only knows.

Climate Change and Ecological Conversion

Can we remain indifferent before the problems associated with such realities as climate change ... Humanity needs a profound cultural renewal; it needs to rediscover those values which can serve as the solid basis for building a brighter future for all. Our present crises—be they economic, food-related, environmental or social—are ultimately also moral crises, and all of them are interrelated. They require us to rethink the path which we are travelling together.

Pope Benedict, 2010

A garden statuette birdbath display of St. Francis is a pleasant, even comforting, image of a man who possessed a certain mystical relationship with the earth, nature, and animals. Through his canticles and other writings, Francis reverently refers to Sir Brother Sun, Sister Moon, Brothers Wind and Air, Sister Water, and Sister, Mother Earth, and proclaims that all creatures on earth and the sea and rivers give praise to God.[1]

Indeed, the scriptures are clear that the human family must look to be good stewards to all of God's creation,[2] a heed that Francis clearly took to heart, long before such terms as "environmentalism," "ecological justice," and "climate change" existed. It should be no surprise, therefore, that in 1979 Pope John Paul II named Francis as the Patron Saint of Ecology, the intersectional study of plant life, animal life, and the environment (e.g., weather, climate, landscapes, human activity).

The Triggering Point of the Industrial Revolution

With the advent of the Industrial Revolution (*c.* 1760–1840s) beginning in Britain and then extending to the rest of Europe, North America, Japan, and other parts of the world, a marked change occurred as society largely moved from an agrarian way of life and manual labor to mass production with the rise of factories, machine power, steam power, chemical production, transport networks, and coal production.[3]

While these advancements had obvious societal benefits, droves of people were steered to urban areas, creating overcrowding and difficult, unsanitary living conditions, which were coupled with the exploitation of factory workers (e.g., underpaid, long hours, child labor, unsafe working environments). This rightly prompted the development of labor unions and child labor laws, laying the foundation for the rights of workers and children.[4] Moreover, it was during this time period Pope Leo XIII wrote his seminal encyclical *Rerum Novarum* (*On the Condition of Workers*), which emphasized the dignity of the person and warned against unbridled capitalism (see Chapter 6).

Outcries in response to the exploitation put in motion gradual actions to protect the rights and dignity of workers, in contrast to lukewarm intentional attentiveness to the environment, to Sister Mother Earth, and particularly with respect to fossil fuel use and its release of greenhouse gases. Fossil fuels (or non-renewable fuels), such as coal, crude oil, and natural gas, are the fossilized remains of animal and plant life from millions of years ago containing high carbon content.[5]

Because coal was the main staple during the Industrial Revolution to power steamboats, trains, and manufacturing, there was an exponential rise of carbon emissions, with large amounts of carbon dioxide released into the atmosphere. As polluted air became trapped and centralized particularly in urban areas, respiratory illnesses became common, leading to early death. Moreover, sewage from factories regularly flowed into waterways, polluting drinking water and causing the spread of diseases such as cholera and typhoid.[6]

While powerful medical advancements have been made on the medical front to deal with asthma, bronchitis, cholera, typhoid, and other diseases, the use of fossil fuels has skyrocketed since the Industrial Revolution, accounting for approximately 80 percent of the world's energy.[7] And as a point of clarification, whether it is water vapor, carbon dioxide, methane, ozone, or nitrous oxide, greenhouse gases are good in and of themselves, in that they are nature's way of allowing sunlight to pass through the atmosphere and snaring the heat to keep the earth warm (i.e., greenhouse effect) as opposed to the gases all escaping into space. Moreover, nature possesses its own monitoring system, regulating these gases as forests, grasslands, wetlands, and oceans to absorb or "drain" these gases through what is called carbon sinks.[8]

Yet, with a high volume of greenhouse emissions coming from electricity and heat, agriculture and land, industry, and transportation, and with China, the United States, India, Russia, and Japan being the five chief users, the emission of carbons and other greenhouse gases far exceeds what nature can handle, meaning the earth is getting hotter.[9] In other words, pollutants are being trapped in the atmosphere where they can linger around for years, even centuries, resulting in what has become known as global warming (or climate change).

This very real phenomenon has been playing havoc with the environment, with more frequent and severe weather, dirtier air, higher wildlife extinction rates, more acidic oceans, higher sea levels, and higher death rates, more acutely affecting the poor worldwide.[10] Pope Francis puts it this way:

> Climate change is a global problem with grave implications: environmental, social, economic, political and for the distribution of goods. It represents one of the principal challenges facing humanity in our day. Its worst impact will probably be felt by developing countries in coming decades. Many of the poor live in areas particularly affected by phenomena related to warming, and their means of subsistence are largely dependent on natural reserves and ecosystemic services such as agriculture, fishing and forestry. They have no other financial activities

or resources which can enable them to adapt to climate change or to face natural disasters, and their access to social services and protection is very limited.[11]

The Pope is not only echoing what climatologists and scientists have warned for years[12] but also asserting that care of the environment falls under the umbrella of the social teachings of the Church. Perhaps even more forcefully, Patriarch Bartholomew, head of the Eastern Orthodox Church, calls humankind's contamination of the earth "a sin against ourselves and a sin against God."[13]

Yet, despite the admonitions, there is a significant cadre of people, in and out of the Church, who are in denial or indifferent about how human activity impacts climate change. This is why, as Pope John Paul II proclaimed in 2001, an "ecological conversion" is needed in order for humankind to better cherish, to better till, and to better honor Sister Mother Earth.[14]

Taking Practical Steps

To move toward that ecological conversion, much can be done both on the international and personal level. To the former, the collective faith community (e.g., Jewish, Buddhist, Hindu, Christian, and Muslim) has made a clear declaration of support for the Paris Climate Agreement.[15] Adopted by 192 parties (i.e., countries, including the European Union) in 2015, the Agreement is a commitment to reduce greenhouse gas emissions with the goal to curb the increase of the global temperature to 2 degrees in this century, even looking to limit it to 1.5 degrees; to hold major emitting countries accountable to decrease climate pollution, strengthening that commitment over time; to encourage "developed" countries to assist "developing" countries in mitigating climate change and adapting to change; and to facilitate a transparent monitoring and reporting system for all countries.[16]

The Paris Agreement followed earlier international environmental and climate initiatives, such as the 1987 Montreal Protocol (environmental accord), the 1992 UN Framework Convention on Climate Change (UNFCCC), and the 1997 Kyoto Protocol (first legally binding treaty), all in the effort to respond to what Pope Francis calls the groans of creation in order to abate the assault on its environment, its land, its animal life, and its people.[17]

Sometimes referred to as the "Green Pope," Benedict XVI recognizes that this abatement requires "[r]espect for the human being and respect for nature are one and the same, but they will both be able to develop and to reach their full dimension if we respect the Creator and his creature in the human being and in nature."[18] And while critics have argued for more ambitious efforts with respect to the Paris Agreement, it is nevertheless a tangible direction toward ecological conversion.[19]

This conversion process can be manifested in any number of personal actionable steps, beginning with being informed and politically aware, and at minimum being familiar with the Church's social teachings on environmental matters.[20] In addition, as outlined in any number of environment and climate-themed websites, one can—where possible—be more economical in water use; recycle, recycle, recycle; look to renewable energy sources (e.g., solar or wind); weatherize; use electric or hybrid model vehicles (i.e., rethinking transportation); protect forestation; plant a tree; use energy-efficient appliances (e.g., wash machines, dryers, etc.); turn lights out when not in use; unplug; use LED lightbulbs; and a host of other things.

In the end, I suspect that as one continues on the road toward ecological conversion, a St. Francis bird bath in the garden will take on a whole different meaning.

Building a Culture of Life

The vocation of the Catholic teacher is an endeavor expressed both in and out of the school building, a vocation that juxtaposes questions, dilemmas, and conundrums, heightening a responsibility to know one's faith, to realize the pedagogical and curricular dynamic, and to be socially and politically astute, all while cultivating a culture of life, one that assumes the possibilities of what it means to travel this path in solidarity.[21]

Indeed, during a worldwide pandemic, the promotion of wearing a mask and social distancing as needed and advocating a vaccine is an effort to preserve life; the support of sensible gun legislation is to secure life; to care and value the unborn child is to protect life; and to nurture the planet is to honor life. All of these are pro-life positions in the effort to build a culture of life, a positionality all Catholic teachers must consider and look to embrace.

Section IV

Know the Spirituality That Enlightens You

Grounded in a Contemplative Way of Being

I believe that the combination of human action from a contemplative center is the greatest art form, one that takes our whole lives to master. When action and contemplation are united, we have beauty, symmetry, and transformation—lives and actions that heal the world by their very presence.

Richard Rohr, 2020

The etymology of the word "sacrament" comes from the Latin *sacramentum* (a solemn oath), from *sacrare* (to consecrate, to make sacred), which derived from the Greek *mysterion* (mystery).[1] Thus, the idea of sacrament or sacramentality suggests a holy moment, a sacred moment, sealed with a vow of commitment. In an ecclesiastical way, this vow takes shape, for example, in the Sacrament of Confirmation, Matrimony, and Holy Orders. It is in these consecrated ceremonies in which, as St. Augustine explains, "the visible form of an invisible grace" is realized as one enters the journey of sacramental thinking and doing, which means being engaged in the sacred within the everydayness of our lives.[2]

In this sacred spirit, Mary Elizabeth Moore, professor emerita of the School of Theology at Boston University, characterizes teaching as a sacramental act, which suggests developing what Thomas H. Groome, professor of theology and religious education, calls a sacramental consciousness.[3] The development of that consciousness as one works in the sacramental act of teaching must be filtered through one's devotion to a regular prayer life. In a certain way, without this devotion, one can miss the most important foundational aspect of this book and what it means to live out the vocation of Catholic teacher.

In the Greek connotation, prayer denotes closeness. Embedded in the simplicity of that closeness is union with a God who illuminates and transforms as we place ourselves "in the hands of God, at his disposition, and listening to his voice in the depths of our hearts,"[4] thus leading to what can be described as "working wonders in a man's [woman's] disposition."[5] While there are many forms of prayer (e.g., adoration and praise, contemplative, thanksgiving, intercession, petition), in the end, time and consistency are fundamental in sustaining a life of prayer, with the assumption that the sincerity of one's heart takes center stage in order for authentic engagement to occur with the living God.[6] In this way, prayer is not simply words; rather, it becomes "a place, an attitude, a stance."[7] And it is in that stance that we realize the proper place of obedience.

Obedience

Derived from the Latin *ob-audire*, obedience means to hear or listen. In the conventional sense, therefore, obedience is the act of listening and complying with rules and regulations. Children should listen and obey parents; employees must submit to their superiors. In those two scenarios, choice, by and large, is not much of an option. As a person of faith, however, the act of obedience is predicated on the notion that I, in fact, have the free will choice to be obedient (listen to God) or not. In other words, God does not demand, but invites us to the table, and it is up to us to pull up a chair.

It is true, however, that many of us associate obedience with a perspective of faith reserved only for those who have made clerical vows. Although likely with fewer restrictions than formally belonging to the clergy or a religious order, many join faith-related lay groups, agreeing to be obedient to their respective precepts. Regardless of the order or group, one likely possesses the desire to join as a response to a prompting from the heart, recognizing the charisms of the group likely harmonizes rightly with one's own temperament, providing a meaningful, communal avenue toward a closer intimate relationship with Jesus.

Of course, there are many people of faith who do not belong to any religious order or lay group. Furthermore, many may not be fully aware of the intent of the spiritual inference of the concept of obedience. Still others do not even care to seriously engage in the notion of "obedience," as the term can provoke negative sentiments, such as the idea of asserting power over the powerless.[8]

Because the concept of obedience may evoke negativity and be misunderstood, many of us are perhaps unaware of its liberating power, and others of us may simply associate it with such concepts as "needing to be good" and a "works" mentality relative to our faith journey. In other words, obedience to extrinsic practices can easily become ends in themselves, resulting in little regard for interior transformation and tempting some of us toward self-righteous behavior. For example, in the Gospels, Jesus, in his encounters with the Pharisees, consistently points out how their own obedience to the law with strict observance to rituals and practices has, in fact, led them away from God. Moreover, in their own "obedience," they not only lost sight of the importance of interior transformation but also became self-righteous and judgmental of others. This observation clearly troubled Jesus.[9]

Yet, in the pure or biblical sense of the concept, obedience is integral to an intimate relationship with Jesus; however, its intent must be wisely grasped in a spiritual context. As the Trappist Thomas Merton (1915–68) points out, "The highest freedom is found in obedience to God. The loss of freedom lies in subjection to the tyranny of automatism, whether in the capriciousness of our own self-will or in the blind dictates of despotism, convention, routine or mere collective inertia."[10] In short, the act of obedience is simply a means, not an end, whereby we choose to listen and let go or surrender to Jesus who has called each of our names.

The implication of making the choice to submit to God in obedience suggests that we understand the deeper meaning of its purpose in our individual choices to, in fact, listen. In other words, we become more aware that the act of obedience means not focusing on oneself but centering on the Lord—a transformative disposition in which a gateway is provided toward deeper interior freedom.

Our becoming toward this freedom naturally draws us onto a path that traverses into the realm of holiness in all that we do (see Rom. 12: 1, 1 Pet. 1:15, Heb. 12:14). The notion of being holy is not some unattainable goal of being perfect; rather, the term suggests being "set apart," realizing a "wholeness" and identity in Christ, which should necessarily be reflected in our way of being as we each strive to live a virtuous life (see Appendix B). Obedience is an essential avenue to ground that life through a contemplative way of being.

To contemplate is to think or reflect deeply over a period of time; it requires an intentionality. For example, particularly when we are faced with major decisions in our lives, we take the time through thoughtful reflection on the pros and cons of a respective decision. We are intentional about the process. Yet, while there is a certain intentionality when contemplation is associated with prayer and engagement with the scriptures, the dynamic of that process is not so much what one does; rather, it is what God does. This, of course, suggests that contemplation is not about you or me; rather, contemplation is a dynamic of staying in the moment with a focus away from oneself, ego, expectations, today, tomorrow.

Contemplative Prayer

During the several years I lived in the state of Utah, I would regularly visit a nearby Trappist monastery and stay for two or three days. The Abbey of Our Lady of the Holy Trinity exuded a humble, sweet spirit with its modest, even outdated, facilities, accompanying the majestic backdrop of the Monte Cristo Mountains to the east and the Wasatch Mountains to the west.[11]

The summer months, with the gentle, warm breeze, perfectly swaying the leafy trees, brought me a tranquil sense of nature; harvest time in the fall brought me the aroma of fresh wheat and the soon-to-be-migrating birds; and springtime brought me a season of new life with a pleasant mix of father winter and sprouting spring. While I enjoyed each season for its own unique richness, I found the winter months most idyllic. The regality of the snow-capped mountains and the thick blanket of snow carpeting the wheat fields, trees, and the one road entering the monastery grounds brought an indescribable sense of magnificence that only can be designed by God. I would bundle up, walk, and simply be silent in the silence of God's heavenly work.

I look back on those times in that particular setting with great affection, forever engraved on my heart. It was a treat to walk the winding roads, spending time in prayer, meditation, and contemplating the majesty of God. In addition, it was nourishing to join the monks in early morning vigils with the chanting of psalms, followed by sitting in silence in the unadorned chapel. It was indeed these sojourns to Holy Trinity that played a weighty part in sealing my commitment to contemplative prayer. And, while I believe people of faith should periodically take the time to be alone with God in such places as a monastery, retreat house, or some other related setting, contemplation is obviously not restricted to such places, nor is it reserved just for those living a cloistered life. To be sure, contemplation can be an integral part of every Christian's daily prayer life.

The contemplative form of prayer begins to unfold when we listen and rest in God from right where we are.[12] In a paradoxical way, the inward journey of this process implies a "dying" to one's self in order to come to an understanding that the kingdom of God, as Henri Nouwen points out, is awakening "ourselves to the God in us."[13] Moreover, Nouwen suggests that when we allow ourselves to grasp the reality of the Lord within, we are allowing God to pervade our heartbeat, our breathing, our thoughts and emotions, and our hearing, seeing, touching, and tasting. In that light, the Trappist Thomas Keating (1923–2018) defines contemplative prayer as,

> The development of one's relationship with Christ to the point of communicating beyond words, thoughts, feelings, and the multiplication of particular acts; a process moving from the simplified

activity of waiting upon God to the ever-increasing predominance of
the Gifts of the Spirit as the source of one's prayer.[14]

Merton furthers Keating's explanation when he underscores, "If we try
to contemplate God without having turned the face of our inner self
entirely in His direction, we will end up inevitably by contemplating
ourselves ... You pray best when the mirror of your soul is empty of
every image except the image of the invisible father."[15] One good place
to turn our face entirely in God's direction is to take the time to meditate
and ponder Scripture. Keating additionally emphasizes that immersion
in the Word leads to understanding while simultaneously letting go of
ordinary ways of knowing.[16] Listening to the Lord in silence and letting
go of our ordinary way of viewing the world and ourselves requires
time and patience.

This letting go does not imply a denial of oneself insofar the
suppression of feelings, emotions, experiences, doubts, fears, and
pleasures. Rather, it suggests an emptying despite the urgings of feelings,
doubts, and fears, while concurrently being open to the prompting of
the spirit. It is in that place where the beginning of wisdom leads to an
infiltration of the heart, often resulting not only in a sweet affirmation of
oneself but also in the presence of a challenge of one's thinking and lens
on the world. In this light, as Merton underscores, "The poet enters into
himself in order to create. The contemplative enters into God in order
to be created."[17] The idea of entering into God in the process of being
created naturally requires a sense of discipline, a spirit of humility, and
a heart in love with God above all else, meaning, as the mystic Julian of
Norwich (*c.* 1342–1430) professes, "In you alone I have everything."[18]

To Live as a Contemplative

Through the daily regularity of prayer with a dispositional stance of
obedience (listening), which includes an attentiveness to meditation on
Scripture (and other faith-inspired works) and a fixed gaze on the God

of life, we come to realize more and more that, indeed, in God we have everything, placing us on the path to live contemplatively. Our lives flow from this inner path, spilling into the enrichment of who we are, how we think, and how we interact in our relationships, suggesting a certain transformative art form, beauty, and symmetry in this way of being.[19] This inner path sustains the work of the Catholic teacher, who realizes that God is personal, but not private; there is a public nature to one's faith.[20]

In other words, to live as a contemplative is to be engaged in that dialectical space, as Cardinal Avery Dulles (1918–2008) emphasizes, where contemplation and action are interwoven; there is no separation between the two.[21] And to reiterate from Chapter 8, Gustavo Gutiérrez would characterize this as the intertwining of reflection on the Word of God, which leads to conversion and then to the Word lived.[22] The nourishment of the inner self produces what Richard Rohr describes as a willing people able to surrender to the transcendent God, thus enabling an opening toward a critical consciousness (or a sacramental consciousness) and transformation.[23]

The dynamic of this dialectical process should contextually filter—as discussed in this text—the recognition of teaching as a vocation; the facilitation of ecumenical, interfaith, and interreligious dialogue; the depth of personalist thought; an understanding of the social teachings of the church and its link to liberation theology; the function of a critical pedagogy in the light of faith; and the process of establishing particular positionalities.

In the end, a contemplative way of being is the cornerstone of a Catholic teacher spirituality, necessarily steering an inner accountability that leads to the conclusion that the work for teaching for social justice with faith, hope, and love is always a work about the other. This cornerstone, I believe, authenticates what it means to be a Catholic teacher.

Afterword

The line "To be a Catholic teacher is to filter that involvement [inside and outside the classroom with students] through a lens shaped by a lived faith" (p. xviii) resonates with me as a lifelong Catholic educator. I am grateful for this opportunity to add some closing remarks about this valuable text for Catholic teachers. Professor Kirylo covers a multitude of topics related to the formation of the Catholic teacher and the school life dilemmas they confront. Beginning his discussion of the teacher's vocation is the Catholic Church's foundational documents on education. Here is where he makes the case for the possibility that a vocation orientation to teaching is appropriate in any school context. He reminds each of us that to be a teacher is a special calling beyond "going to work" or "having a job." The act of teaching involves more than a professional aspiration. The relationship between teacher and learner should be more covenant than contract.

This relational foundation is followed by an attractive interpretation of liberation theology that leads to an evolving critical pedagogy. Liberation theology is often associated with its political activity, but it is the "preferential option for the poor" where Kirylo places his emphasis. The agenda of the Latin American Bishops' Conference of 1979 in Puebla, Mexico, was heavily influenced by Gustavo Gutiérrez's action orientation for liberation theology that focuses on serving the other. An event and a scholar regularly referenced as profoundly impactful to Pope Francis's core beliefs. Poverty and its by-products often hold students hostage to a negative performance trajectory. The liberation teacher uses a critical pedagogy that examines these circumstances and intervenes wherever and however possible.

Critical pedagogy intersects with my work, as the further explanation will convey. Both critical pedagogy and contemplative leadership presume that education is value laden. As the eminent educational researcher John Goodlad states, teaching is a moral activity.[1] Critical implies that the teacher is not a neutral utilitarian fonctionnaire but a person ("I") engaging with the student ("Thou") in a meaningful transformative learning process.

Kirylo's text does not shy away from a Catholic teacher's uncomfortable confrontation with contemporary dilemmas, and he offers direction with his discussion of positionality. As the text reaches its climax, he presents contemplative living as the culmination of his presentation on the Catholic teacher's formation. Professor Kirylo carefully puts in place the pieces of his argument that contemplative living is the coherent worldview and lifestyle for a Catholic teacher.

After reading *The Catholic Teacher: Teaching for Social Justice with Faith, Hope and Love,* my worldview for the Catholic teacher was confirmed. My research runs a parallel course directed toward the Catholic school leader, whom I regularly describe as the teacher of teachers or lead teacher. In 1993, I began to more intensely reflect on the distinctive role of the Catholic school leader as I had just completed a private university's doctoral program in educational administration and was a Catholic school principal.

While the program was excellent in many respects, it did not address the context of the Catholic school and its unique mission. Contemplative leadership was my response to this missing content, a model that integrates a Catholic worldview and reflective practice with a school leader's decision making.[2] The Catholic school leader's worldview is an educational philosophy (critical reflection) shaped by Church teachings, tradition, and virtues. Essential to contemplative leadership is the character of that leader formed within key communities where virtue is developed and nourished.

In the contemplative leadership model, the result is a Catholic school community depicted as a faith learning internship. Within that faith learning community all adults share a responsibility to be a faith witness with teachers in a key role through their direct and extensive contact with students. Upon reflection, I could readily describe life within the faith internship community as Kirylo's contemplative living. Coherence is essential within contemplative leadership as values and beliefs are translated into actions while creating meaning (e.g., What is a good teacher? Good student? Good parent?). The school leader sets the stage for a faith internship community—contemplative living— through the school's curriculum and community-building activities.[3] The contemplative leader's personal credibility as a faith-filled witness and their communication skills focused on a shared community vision make the faith internship both practical and transformative.

Due to Professor Kirylo and my shared purpose for teachers, contemplative living, it is possible to find overlap and complementary concepts presented within his text and my writings. While my work focused directly on Catholic schools and their community members, Professor Kirylo challenges Catholic teachers in all educational settings to embrace the vocation inherent in the teaching profession wherever one teaches. His point is to emphasize the Catholic worldview that prioritizes relationships with students gifted through their creation in God's image. His acknowledgment of the Divine in each student makes his focus on personalism an obvious disposition for teachers. If the Divine in each person is validated, as his discussion states, then the social teachings of the Church provide the liberation framework for action that recognizes the struggles students face whether academic, economic, or social.

In the final analysis, if one has read with a discerning eye, there is a great deal educators can draw from this text, realizing that foundational to teaching for social justice in faith, hope, and love is one that is grounded in a contemplative way of being.

Merylann "Mimi" J. Schuttloffel, Professor Emerita
The Catholic University of America

Appendix A
Two Major Splits in the Church

The Great Schism

When Constantine worked to move the capital of the Roman Empire to Byzantium in 330 CE, he renamed the seat of the "New Rome" Constantinople (after his name, now modern-day Istanbul). This move set a historic split between the East (Constantinople) and West (Rome), not only as a geographic divide but also through language, as in the East, Greek was dominant, while in the West, Latin was. Moreover, the Church in the East began a gradual process to theologically break away from the Church in the West, ultimately paving the road to the Great Schism of 1054.[1]

Among other differences, the Church in the East favored the use of leavened bread for the Eucharistic celebration, while the West was in favor of unleavened bread; the Church in the East was disturbed with an inclusion of the *filioque* (and the son) clause ("the Holy Spirit proceeds from the Father and the Son," as opposed to proceeding just from the Father as was the original teaching) in the Nicene Creed; and, the East even argued that clergy should have beards, as was the case for Christ and his apostles.[2] While those aforementioned differences were contentious in and of themselves, the major triggering event that prompted the Schism occurred when Pope Leo IX looked to excommunicate the Patriarch of Constantinople, Cerularius, who did not recognize the Papacy as head of the Church. In turn, intensifying the conflict, Cerularius looked to excommunicate Leo IX.[3]

Over the centuries, however, the relationship between the Church in the East and the West has thawed, establishing common understandings. For example, Pope Paul VI and Ecumenical Patriarch Athenagoras I of Constantinople agreed at an historic event in 1965 to express regret on both sides between the two churches, particularly between Leo IX and Cerularius "and remove both from memory and from the midst of the Church the sentences of excommunication ... and they commit these excommunications to oblivion."[4] Moreover, though reconciliation attempts have been made, particularly through the Councils of Lyons II (1274) and Florence (1439) to unify the Eastern and Western Churches regarding the *filioque* clause, it still remains a point of contention, albeit within a present-day conciliary space. Because God the Father and God the son share the same divine nature, the issue surrounding the clause is more of a question of semantics for many.[5]

The Protestant Reformation

While the Roman Catholic Church continued to grow after the Great Schism, it was not without a continuation of internal and external conflict, which notably erupted in the sixteenth century. Martin Luther (1483–1546), an Augustinian monk and ordained priest, sharply committed to his faith, struggled with the direction of the Church, especially indulgences and the authoritative role of the Papacy. Luther viewed scripture as the sole authority of church teachings, with justification for salvation based on faith alone.

Of course, the Catholic Church embraces the teachings of scripture, yet along with tradition and church authority as an integral part of those teachings. Moreover, the Catholic Church views that one is justified by faith, but for the faith to be authentic, it is manifested in good works. A discussion of detailed concepts related to justification by faith, salvation, the place of good works, and the role of scripture is beyond the scope of inquiry here, except to say it remains a continuous multilayered discussion among Christian circles.

With respect to the former, Luther indeed had a point as he observed institutional abuse when it came to the practice of indulgences, a practice through which one could reduce punishment for sin for a departed loved one in Purgatory or reduce punishment for oneself.[6] This practice is conducted through good works, extra prayer, visitation to a shrine, or monetary donations to the church or related affiliations.

Obviously a highly complex, controversial theological configuration, the intersection of purgatory and indulgences came to a head in the 1500s, as abuse was evident, particularly as it lined the pockets of the institutional Church and individual clergy alike. In this collective light and as an act of protest, in 1517 Martin Luther nailed ninety-five theses on a chapel door at the University of Wittenberg.[7] The posting of the document marked the advent of another major split within the Church: the Protestant Reformation.[8] Protestants, as they later became called, did not want to have anything to do with the Roman Church.

The Counter-Reformation (Catholic Reform)

While the Catholic Church was already in the process of its own spiritual and theological renewal prior to Martin Luther's protest, the Protestant Reformation accelerated the urgency of that process with the Church's Counter-Reformation (or Catholic Reform), which was particularly punctuated with the convening of the Council of Trent (1545–63). The Council affirmed Papal authority and "dogmas of the divine validity of the seven sacraments, the hierarchical nature of the Church, the divine institution of the priesthood, the traditional teaching on transubstantiation (Jesus's real presence in the communion), and the sacrificial character of the Mass."[9]

Moreover, the sale of indulgences was terminated (decreed by Pope Pius V in 1567), bishops were required to live in the diocese they were overseeing, better training and oversight of priests was installed, and new religious orders were established, including the Society of Jesus (Jesuits). Finally, a new injection of spirituality, which attracted the devout laity, emerged from the thought and practice of St. Ignatius of Loyola (founder of the Jesuits) (1491–1556), Peter Canisius (1521–97), and Teresa of Avila (1515–82), among others, as well as the encouragement of Eucharistic adoration and more often receiving Communion.[10]

Since the beginning of its formation, the Catholic Church has been fraught with struggles from within and without, particularly marked by the Great Schism and the Protestant Reformation. Because of differing theological perspectives as well as differences regarding church hierarchal frameworks, clerical formations and functions, the role of the laity, and forms of church service and worship, the Christian Church has largely remained splintered as a corporate body.[11]

However, the modern-day ecumenical movement, traceable back to 1844 with the formation of the Young Men's Christian Association (YMCA), the establishment of the World Council of Churches in 1948, and Vatican II (1962–5), has been a powerful force in finding unity, despite differences, within the Christian Church (see Chapter 2).

Appendix B
The Concept of Virtue

Virtue, as a concept, goes as far back to Plato's *Republic*, in which it is associated with moral living and public life.[1] Aristotle not only linked virtue to happiness but also suggested that being virtuous is not something that comes naturally but rather is cultivated through practice and habit. Virtuousness, therefore, becomes a character state, manifested in the choices one makes in conducting acts of virtue.[2]

In that light and deriving from Greek thought, the virtues—more commonly called the cardinal virtues—emerge: prudence, justice, fortitude, and temperance (see Appendix C). The term "cardinal" is significant, as it is derived from the Latin *cardo*, meaning "pivot" or "hinge," thus suggesting that these "pivotal" cardinal virtues are what all other virtues hinge in order to live a moral or virtuous life.[3]

St. Augustine richly furthered our understanding of virtue in the fifth century, reasoning that while from one perspective he saw virtue as an established characteristic of the soul, innately impacting morally right action, from another perspective, he viewed virtue as a deliberate act or choice in which one rightly and properly lives. From either perspective, however, Augustine was clear about the link between the Christian life and the place of the cardinal virtues. But Augustine placed chief importance on what are known as the theological virtues (faith, hope, and love).[4]

As Thomas Aquinas puts it, the concepts of faith, hope, and love are theological virtues because of their eternal significance and because they are "infused in us by God alone."[5] Faith is naturally associated with one's belief system, often expressed in one's religion or spirituality, requiring conviction, commitment, and trust.[6] It is reasonable to assume, therefore, that the authenticity of one's faith is determined through the manifestation to one's commitment to a prayer life (Mt. 6:6, Lk. 6:12), to the common good (Mt. 7:12, Phil. 2:3-4), and a more just and loving world (Lk. 4: 16-19, 1 Jn 4: 11-12).

And while faith is naturally linked to things of the spirit and religious belief systems, there is also the idea of faith expressed in the context of possessing a fundamental faith in the human family, which is revealed in how we relate with one another. And while hope is a concept that is viewed as a theological virtue, it is also a necessary psychological element that provides for human beings a sense of purpose in order to live meaningfully. That is, "Hope is the presupposition behind the human 'will to live.'"[7]

The theological virtue of love grounded St. Augustine's thought, as evident in his famous proclamation "Love, and do what you will."[8] In other words, Augustine understood that a deep love for God is spiritually transformative, naturally illuminating a whole new way as to how one views oneself, powerfully impacting a willingness to live a life of faith. This suggests that acts of goodness in and of themselves are not what make those acts virtuous but, rather, it is the love that drives those acts that enables the radiance of virtue. Stated another way, doing "whatever you will" is driven by a freedom found through obedience in a love relationship with a God who sets us free.

Appendix C
The Cardinal Virtues
(And Eschatological Virtues)

Because he saw it as linked to the intellect, Thomas Aquinas viewed prudence as the first cardinal virtue, which enables us to make judgments with respect to right and wrong, as well as the kinds of willful decisions we all make. Particularly when requesting wise counsel from others, especially when it comes to complex decisions, seeking prudence allows us to reduce the possibility of making an error. Second to prudence, according to Aquinas, is the cardinal virtue of justice, which emphasizes human rights.[1] Based on earlier Catholic social teaching (i.e., *Rerum Novarum* [On the Condition of Workers, 1891], *Quadragesimo Anno* [On the Fortieth Year, 1931]), justice was central to the documents of Vatican II (1962–5), particularly illuminated with the advent of liberation theology (see Chapters 6–8).

Although countless other examples exist linking the scriptures to social justice, it was Martin Luther King Jr. who, in his famous 1963 "I Have a Dream" speech, drew from the book of Amos (5:24-27), when he proclaimed in oratorical magnificence that devotees of civil rights will not be satisfied until "justice rolls down like waters, and righteousness like a mighty stream." Indeed, social justice is about the cultivation of the common good in which all of God's people can equitably, justly, and rightly participate in a civil society.

Aquinas contends fortitude (or courage) is the third cardinal virtue: despite the various obstacles, fears, or challenges we each face in life, fortitude provides for us the strength to carry on. Particularly as it relates to defense of one's faith in the midst of persecution, fortitude can also be characterized as a gift of the Holy Spirit. The final cardinal virtue is temperance, which, according to Aquinas, is manifested in how we exhibit self-control regarding our carnal desires (e.g., appetite for food, drink, sex). In other words, temperance provides for us the ability to withhold from excess or abuse.[2]

In addition to the cardinal and theological virtues (faith, hope, and love), there are also eschatological virtues (gratitude, humility, vigilance, serenity, and joy), which in theological terms are given by the Holy Spirit, suggesting there are certain dispositions, values, and times in which these virtues help us to live a moral, ethical, and righteous life. Naturally, however, the concept of virtue intersects with moral development and had a clear impact on the thinking of Erik Erikson, Jean Piaget, and Lawrence Kohlberg, who have significantly contributed to how we grow, develop, process, and learn to deal with the world around us.[3]

Notes

Preface

1 My father, who was the son of Polish parents, was originally from Boston, and my mother was born and raised in Holland. They met during the Second World War, as my father was part of the Army brigade that liberated Maastricht from Nazi tyranny. Shortly after the war they married and stayed in Europe, ending up in Italy, where I was born.

2 Chittister, 2010.

3 Mt. 25:40.

4 See Mt. 19:21.

5 Hill, 1987, p. 1013.

6 Nouwen, 1984, p. xiii.

7 Rohr, O.F.M., 1987a. Romero (1979) puts it this way: It's amusing: This week I received accusations from both extremes—from the extreme right, that I am a communist; from the extreme left, that I am joining the right. I am not with the right or with the left. I am trying to be faithful to the word that the Lord bids me preach, to the message that cannot change, which tells both sides the good they do and the injustices they commit (p. 163).

8 See Lk. 4: 18-19.

9 A day after Romero's assassination, a journalist reported that Romero had earlier asserted, "I have often been threatened with death. But I must say that as a Christian, I do not believe in death without resurrection. If they kill me I will rise again in the Salvadoran people" (p. 190). While that quotation is quite moving and even right on in its spirit, it is believed in some circles that the citation was an invention by the journalist (Eisenbrandt, 2017).

10 Mk 8:27-29.

11 Gutiérrez, 1984, pp. 46, 51.

12 de Cepeda y Ahumada, 2007, p. 53.

Introduction

1   Leean, 1988.
2   In order to make some distinctions, it may be helpful to briefly point out that though *religion* and *spirituality* can be related, *spirituality* does not depend on *religion*, which is the social or organized means by which people can express *spirituality*. In broad terms, spirituality can be characterized as one's intrinsic link to something bigger or transcendent to oneself. And while *spirituality* exists without the structure of *religion*, authentic *religion* cannot be without *spirituality* (Chandler, Holden & Kolander, 1992l; Grim, 1994). In the context of a conversation on the transcendent, *faith* encompasses conviction, commitment, and trust (Dulles, 1977), and *theology* is the "science of God," which is a process of reflecting on the human experience in the light of *faith* (Morneau, 1983; O'Collins & Farrugia, 1991).
3   Helminiak, 1987; Warren, 1988; Kolander & Chandler, 1990; Nouwen, 2016.
4   Groome, 2019.
5   With respect to my discussions on the social teachings of the Church, liberation theology, critical pedagogy, neoliberalism, and gun control, I draw portions from my respective books: Kirylo, 2011; Kirylo & Boyd, 2017; Kirylo & Aldridge, 2019; Kirylo, 2021.
6   Parts of these respective chapters collectively draw from my work, Kirylo, 2011; Kirylo & Boyd, 2017; Kirylo & Aldridge, 2019; Kirylo, 2021.
7   Parts of this chapter is adapted from my work (Kirylo, 2021).
8   Fernando Llort, n.d.

Chapter 1

1   Lk 24:51-53.
2   Acts 2:2-3.
3   The name of the day itself is derived from the Greek word *pentecoste*, meaning fiftieth. Thus, forty days after the crucifixion and resurrection, and ten days after the ascension. The number fifty days is no coincidence, as it is equivalent to the number of days of the Jewish holiday of Shavout (feast of weeks), which is fifty days or seven weeks after Passover. The

commemoration of Shavuot is rooted in the ancient festival of the grain harvest and when the Torah was given on Mount Sinai, which occurred seven weeks after the exodus from Egypt (see: https://www.catholicnewsagency. com/news/everything-you-need-to-know-about-pentecost-78932).

4 Acts 2:5-41.

5 See Jn 21:15-17. Moreover, and more particularly in recognizing Peter as the first pope, the Church looks to Mt. 16:18, which states, "And so I say to you, you are Peter, and upon this rock I will build my church, and the gates of the netherworld shall not prevail against it." Depending on a respective perspective regarding the interpretation of this particular verse, the term "rock" is disputed with respect to who Jesus was referring to (i.e., himself or Peter). It is beyond the scope here to enter that discussion; however, see here for a brief explanation: https://www.catholic.com/tract/origins-of-peter-as-pope.

6 See Acts 11:26.

7 In citing Ignatius of Antioch, Pope Benedict, writes, "'Wherever Jesus Christ is', he [Ignatius] said, 'there is the Catholic Church' (*Smyrnaeans*, 8: 2). And precisely in the service of unity to the Catholic Church, the Christian community of Rome exercised a sort of primacy of love: 'The Church which presides in the place of the region of the Romans, and which is worthy of God, worthy of honour, worthy of the highest happiness … and which presides over love, is named from Christ, and from the Father … '" (*Romans*, Prologue) (see http://www.vatican.va/content/benedict-xvi/en/audiences/2007/documents/hf_ben-xvi_aud_20070314.html). Moreover, when the community gathered for worship, the sharing of bread and wine was the focal point of the celebration, which Ignatius called the Eucharist (thanksgiving) (MacCulloch, 2010).

8 According to Eusebius of Caesarea (260/265–339/340 CE), who, although somewhat of a controversial fourth-century historian of church history (or ecclesiastical history), recorded that the letters of Ignatius were written to the Churches of Ephesus, Magnesia, Tralli, Rome, Philadelphia, Smyrna, and one to Polycarp, who was the Bishop of Smyrna (see: https://www. catholicculture.org/culture/library/view.cfm?recnum=3836; http://www. vatican.va/content/benedict-xvi/en/audiences/2007/documents/hf_ben-xvi_aud_20070314.html). St. Polycarp (*c.* 69–*c.*155), St. Clement of Rome, and St. Ignatius of Antioch are considered chief of all Apostolic Fathers,

meaning they had some kind of personal contact with the original twelve disciples of Jesus (see: https://www.newadvent.org/cathen/01637a.htm).

9   See Acts 16:37; 22:25-28.

10   United States Conference of Catholic Bishops (2011). The New American Bible (Revised Edition) Commentary before The Letter to the Romans, p. 1252. World Catholic Press (A Division of Catholic Book Publishing Corp.): New Jersey.

11   When the Church incorporates "Roman" to such items as the missal, rite, or curia, it is referring to the Diocese of Rome. And while the Roman (or Latin) rite and tradition is the largest within the Catholic Church, there are other distinct rites and traditions in the Church which generally reflect the Eastern rite, such as the Armenian, Byzantine, Caldean (East Syrian), Coptic, Ethiopian, Marionite, and West Syrian who acknowledge the Bishop of Rome, the Pope, as the head of the entire Catholic Church (Whitehead, 1996; New World Encyclopedia, 2019).

12   Whitehead, 1996; Ray, 2005; MacCulloch, 2010; *Online Etymology Dictionary*, n.d.(a).

13   Ong, 1990. While Ong's reflections on the term "catholic" was in the context of its link to Catholic institutions of higher learning, there were clear generalizations that can be made relative to his argument.

14   Ibid., p. 2.

15   Ibid., pp. 2–3.

16   Roccasalvo, 2013.

17   Ong, 1990, p. 8.

Chapter 2

1   Jn 17:21.

2   See, for example, Acts 15:1-29, 1 Cor. 1:10-17, and Jas 4:1-12.

3   Stefon, 2012.

4   Ibid.

5   Ibid.

6   Ibid.

7   World Council of Churches, n.d.

8   Cogley, 2020.

9   Jn 17:21.
10 Decree on Ecumenism (Unitatis Redintegratio) (1964). Part 1.
11 Online Etymology Dictionary (n.d., b). The idea of ecumenism is no
    small matter given the history of the Christian Church. Whether it be
    the 1054 Great Schism, the Protestant Reformation, and other skirmishes
    in the Church, the divisiveness was wrought with a trail of inquisitions,
    fighting, bloodshed, death, burnings at the stake, torture, and corruption.
    Though there still remains lingering tensions and misunderstandings
    among Christian groups to this day, there is not near that raw violence of
    yesteryear.
12 Unitatis Redintegratio (Decree on Ecumenism) (1964) (Part 8). In 1995
    with his release of the encyclical *Ut Unum Sint* (That They Be One) (On
    Commitment to Ecumenism), Pope John Paul II elaborates more deeply
    on the meaning of ecumenism as a result of what came out of Vatican II.
    He reiterates the primacy of prayer, brotherhood, solidarity, and that
    ecumenism is the way of the church in order to restore unity among
    Christians. In addition to striving unity among Christian groups during
    his pontificate, John Paul II also advocated dialogical exchanges among
    non-Christian Religions and traditions. Following Pope John Paul II,
    Pope Benedict and Pope Francis, too, have made ecumenism a central
    part of their respective papacies.
13 Poggioli, 2016.
14 In his book, *Catholics and Protestants: What Can We Learn from
    Each Other?* (2017), Peter Kreeft, philosophy professor and convert to
    Catholicism, reminds his audience that Martin Luther's intention was not
    to start a new Church; rather, his intention was to reform the Church,
    and, as such, fundamentally making Luther's efforts "*God's* reformation"
    (p. 116, author emphasis). In that light, therefore, as Kreeft, asserts, "Most
    Christians, Protestants as well as Catholics, do not know that the majority
    of Lutherans in the world seek *and expect* the Reformation to end and
    reunion with Rome to succeed some day" (p. 17, author's emphasis).
15 Chryssavgis, 2014.
16 Amin, 2019, para. 4.
17 See: http://legacy.archchicago.org/departments/ecumenical/relations.htm
18 Poggioli, 2015.
19 Nostra Aetate, 1965.

20 Ut Unum Sint(On Commitment to Ecumenism), 1995.

21 Pope John Paul II, 1986.

22 Nostra Aetate, 1965 (Part 3).

23 Pope Francis, 2020a.

24 See also two other encyclicals by Pope Francis, *Evangelii Gaudium* (The Joy of the Gospel) (2014) and *Laudato Si'* (Praise be to You) (2015).

25 Al-Marashi, 2021; Harlan & Loveluck, 2021.

26 Laity, n.d.

27 Lumen Gentium, 1964. Also, affirming the role of the Laity is the Vatican II document *Apostolicam Actuositatem* (Decree on the Apostolate of the Laity) (1965), which states that one's union with Christ and through Baptism and strengthened through Confirmation the Lord Himself assigns the laity to the apostolate and are "consecrated for the royal priesthood and the holy people" (cf. 1 Pet. 2:4-10) (Ch. 1, para 3).

Chapter 3

1   Mother Teresa Center, n.d.

2   Ibid.

3   Ibid.

4   Mother Teresa, 1979, para 6–7.

5   The white sari signifies truth and purity and the three blue borders denote the vows of the Order (poverty, obedience, chastity, with a commitment to serve the poorest of the poor). A cross which is displayed on the left shoulder suggests that the Christ on the cross is central to the heart. (Das, 2015).

6   Saint Francis, 2015, para. 20.

7   Mother Teresa, 2015.

8   Bowman, 2015.

9   See The Full Story | Xavier University of Louisiana (xula.edu).

10 To be sure, while the Catholic Church has conducted some good work in the effort to be more inclusive, it is common knowledge that it still has a way to go when it comes to working with Black Catholics and women. For example, see here: https://www.msnbc.com/opinion/black-catholics-have-right-be-frustrated-church-ignores-racism-n1284598,

and here: https://www.ncronline.org/news/vatican/synod-ends-calling-womens-inclusion-catholic-leadership-duty-justice.

11 It was at this writing that Dr. Farmer unexpectedly and sadly passed away in Rwanda.

12 Kirylo & Boyd, 2017.

13 Goizueta, 1995; Griffin & Block, 2013, p. 6.

14 World Central Kitchen, n.d.

15 Andrés, 2019.

16 The February 2021 takeover by Myanmar's military toppled the landslide elected civilian administration of Aung San Suu Kyi, the 1991 Nobel Peace Prize recipient. The claim for the coup was alleged election fraud, though there was no evidence to support that assertion. In addition, it was claimed that Suu Kyi violated state secret protocols, along with other charges. Critics claim charges against Suu Kyi were politically motived, with many countries condemning the military takeover. Thus, the large numbers of protestors took to the streets, including government workers, bank officials, attorneys, teachers, and students (Cuddy, 2021).

17 Thawng, 2021, para. 3.

18 Al Jazeera, 2021; Bowling, 2021; Glatz, 2021.

19 Pope Francis, 2021, para. 4.

20 Fedele, 2020.

21 Fialka, 2003.

22 Pope Francis, 2013, para 6.

Chapter 4

1 In Catholic lexicon the "religious" life in a more formal sense is when a man or a woman decides to join a religious order as a "brother" or "sister" (or nun) generally taking the vows of poverty, chastity, and obedience. Of course, many priests belong to religious orders, such as the Jesuits or Franciscans, who can be assigned to various parts of the world as opposed to diocesan priests who live, work, and stay in certain geographic areas (i.e., diocese). And while diocesan priests take the vows of chastity and obedience (i.e., to the area bishop), they don't take the vow of poverty.

2 Particularly prior to Vatican II and for some time after the landmark Council, an emphasis on the favored status and "holiness" of the clergy over the spiritual "inferiority" or lowliness of the laity was a common thought pattern perpetuated by the Church (Eisenbrandt, 2017).

3 Gravissimum Educationis (1965). The document also accentuates that parents are the principal educators of their children, and, moreover, highlights the unique mission of Catholic schools, colleges, and universities. It also must be noted that an earlier encyclical by Pope Pius XI, *Divini Illius Magistri* (On Christian Education) (1929), emphasizes the importance of teachers and the necessity for them to not only be well prepared and knowledgeable but also that teachers are those who possess a deep love for young people.

4 Buck, 1950, para. 1–2.

5 Lay Catholics in schools: Witnesses to faith (1982) (part 37).

6 Pope Paul VI, 1970.

7 Lay Catholics in schools: Witnesses to faith (1982), (part 21).

8 Kirylo, 2021.

9 Arthur, 2015.

10 Darder, 2016, p. 19.

11 Pope Francis, 2020b.

Chapter 5

1 Freire, 1998a, p. 64.

2 Wherever he traveled, Maurin was fond of saying, "There is a man in France called Emmanuel Mounier. He wrote a book called The Personalist Manifesto. You should read that book" (Zwick, M., Zwick, L., 2005, p. 115). Born in Grenoble, France, near the French Alps, Mounier abandoned his medical studies and sought the guidance of Jacques Chevalier, leading him to the work of Henri Bergson, Charles Péguy, and Jacques Maritain, among others. And during the first half of the twentieth century, Paris, Munich, and Lublin were critical higher learning centers in Europe where personalists particularly gathered. This was during the time frame in which Europe was confronted with economic disarray, political and moral confusion, a traditionalist institutional church, and

in which the masses of people found little comfort in the materialism and individualist roots of the bourgeois, and reacted to the determinism, rationalism, and the absolute idealism of Georg Hegel. As a response to this European reality (c. between the First World War and the Second World War), Emmanuel Mounier, as part of the Parisian group, emerged as a leader of personalist thought with his founding of the journal *Esprit* (founded 1932 along with Jacques Maritain and Gabriel Marcel) (Inglis, 1959; Sawchenko, 2013; Williams & Bengtsson, 2016).

3   Day, 1945 (para. 1).

4   It is worth to point out that personalism is not a singular system of thinking or a solitary attitude but rather a philosophy (Mounier, 1952), making it a challenging concept to define because there are a variety of "personalisms." For example, there are strands of personalism that are European, North American, Latin American, Eastern, and African, representing an array of personalistic branches that include realistic personalists and idealistic personalists (subdivided into personal idealists, ethical personalists, absolutistic personalists, and panpsychistic personalists) (Burford, n.d., Williams & Bengtsson, 2016). It is also worth pointing out that in drawing from the works of Albert C. Knudson (*The Philosophy of Personalism. A Study in the Metaphysics of Religion* (1969)), and Hubert E. Langan (*The Philosophy of Personalism and Its Educational Applications* (1935)), De Tavernier (2009) asserts that personalism first emerged on the scene from the thought of Plato and Plotinus. And while personalism can be traced to the early Greeks, it is also true that it is linked to ancient Hindu philosophy and Confucianism (Burford, n.d.). However, within all the strands of personalism, the centrality of the person, the uniqueness of personhood, and the connection among persons is elemental. And while personalism is not only linked to the metaphysical and possesses an integral link to the spiritual and belief in God, this does not suggest that all personalists are theists or believers in a god(s) (Williams & Bengtsson, 2016).

5   Inglis, 1959; Sawchenko, 2013; Williams & Bengtsson, 2016.

6   Pope Francis, 2020a.

7   As the Franciscan Richard Rohr (2013) puts it, individualism is that in which one retreats into self to find ultimate truth in an egocentric way that says, "I alone will be my reference point" (p. 2).

8   Mounier, 1952.

9   Roberts, 2000, p. 45.

10 Inglis, 1959; Eneau, 2008; Sawchenko, 2013; Williams & Bengtsson, 2016.

11 Sawchenko, 2013; Williams & Bengtsson, 2016.

12 Mounier, 1995, para. 7.

13 Mounier, 1962, pp. 182–3.

14 Mounier, 1938, p. 7.

15 Mounier, 1962.

16 Komonchak, Collins & Lane, 1987.

17 Kirylo, 2011.

18 Ibid.

19 Cunningham, 1987; Edwords, 1989, 2008; Kirylo, 2011.

20 Williams & Bengtsson, 2016.

21 To hear the original by Reverend William Holmes Borders, Sr., see: https://www.youtube.com/watch?v=L-6JcyLrmHE from the early 1940s. Later, in the early 1970s, the Reverend Jesse Jackson released his rendition of the work as narrated on his appearance on Sesame Street, seen here: https://worshipwords.co.uk/i-am-somebody-jesse-jackson-chicago-illinois-usa/.

22 Pope Francis, 2020a, pp. 46, 49, 53, 59.

23 Buber, 1958.

24 Freire, 1994.

25 Day, 1963, 1997, p. 215.

Chapter 6

1   Lk. 4:16-22.

2   Ibid.

3   Of course, there are other scripture passages that ground the social teachings of the Church, which, in addition to those highlighted in this chapter, consider the following: Mic. 6:8, Isa. 1:17, Jer. 22:3, Amos 5:24, Mt. 19:21, Mt. 25:35-36, and Acts 2:45.

4   United States Conference of Catholic Bishops, 2011.

5   Donovan, 1974; Ellsberg, 2012. For a descriptive account on how the indigenous populations were treated, see *The Devastation of the Indies: A Brief Account* (1974) by Bartolomé de Las Casas.

6   As a matter of historical context when in the 1400s the Spanish Crown
    (and later the Portuguese) set out to cross the Atlantic to explore
    what was new lands to them, the crusade of Spain and the mission
    of the Church became one and the same. That is, the establishment
    of a hierarchical feudal system of the mother country appeared to
    be successful, fostering a newly developed social order as a form of
    Christendom, a concept that is attributed to the era of Constantine at
    the beginning of the fourth century, whereby Constantine, as an act
    of policy, united the secular state with the church (Muggeridge, 1980;
    Dussel, 1981; Nunez, 1985; Berryman, 1987). Thus, "Christianity is the
    Christian religion. 'Christendom' is a cultural reality. The former is a
    religion, the latter is a cultural totality which derives its basic orientation
    from Christianity … Christendom was not just an ecclesiastical unity;
    it was also a military and economic unity" (Dussel, 1976, pp. 70–1). In
    that light, therefore, Latin American Christendom created ecclesiastical,
    cultural, economic, and political interdependence, which characterizes
    as "an imposition of medieval, Spanish, and Roman Christianity, but
    not an evangelization that would convert people to New Testament
    Christianity" (Nunez, 1985, p. 19). As a result of an ecclesiastical and
    state unity with its invasion to the "new world," it took down the Mayan,
    Aztec, and Inca civilizations. Within a year after the arrival of Cortes, the
    Aztec Empire was gone. Moreover, and though they lasted a little longer
    than the Aztecs, the Inca Empire fell at the hands of Pizarro and his
    Spanish soldiers in three years (Van Doren, 1991). Other than the voices
    of a minority of clergy, the Church was virtually silent about the death
    and destruction that occurred because they (the Church) "sometimes
    doubted that the natives actually possessed souls, but never doubted
    that—in cases of resistance to the Catholic faith—death was better than
    life without Christ" (Smith, 1991, p. 12). These early actions by the
    Spanish and Portuguese established the beginnings for contemporary
    oppressive conditions in Latin America. No longer called "Indians" and
    "conquerors," the parties involved are now called "the poor" and the
    "wealthy landowners" (Dussel, 1981; Gutiérrez, 1993).
7   Donovan, 1974; Ellsberg, 2012.
8   Ellsberg, 2012, para. 12 & 13.
9   United States Conference of Catholic Bishops, 2011.

10   Along with Bartolomé de Las Casas, Bishop of Chiapas (1544–7),
      Antonio de Valdivieso, Bishop of Nicaragua (1544–50), Cristobal de
      Pedraza, Bishop of Honduras (1545–83), Pablo de Torres, Bishop of
      Panama (1547–54), and Juan del Valle, Bishop of Popayan (1548–60)
      were also powerful voices for the human rights of the indigenous
      populations (Dussel, 1981).
11   Leo XIII, 1942, p. 6.
12   Dorr, 1983.
13   With a 90th anniversary commemoration of *Rerum Novarum*, Pope John
      Paul II released his encyclical *Laborem Exercens* (On Human Work)
      (1981), and for the 100th anniversary, he released *Centesimus Annus* (The
      Hundredth Year) (1991).
14   Smith, 1991.
15   Ibid., p. 85.
16   Gremillion, 1976.
17   Sigmund, 1988; Hennelly, 1990.
18   O'Brien & Shannon, 1977.
19   For a comprehensive list of Papal, Vatican, and USCCB documents
      relative to CST, see: https://www.usccb.org/beliefs-and-teachings/what-
      we-believe/catholic-social-teaching/foundational-documents.
20   United States Conference of Catholic Bishops, 2011, para. 2.
21   Smith, 1991.

Chapter 7

1   Three days after his election, Pope Francis stood in the Paul VI Audience
     Hall in Rome to address the media, and explained the choosing of his
     papal name:

> At the election I had the archbishop emeritus of Sao Paulo next to
> me. He is also prefect emeritus of the Congregation for the Clergy,
> Cardinal Claudio Hummes [O.F.M.]: a dear, dear friend. When
> things were getting a little 'dangerous', he comforted me. And
> then, when the votes reached the two-thirds, there was the usual
> applause because the Pope had been elected. He hugged me and
> said: 'Do not forget the poor.' And that word stuck here [tapping
> his forehead]; the poor, the poor. Then, immediately in relation

to the poor I thought of Francis of Assisi. Then I thought of war,
while the voting continued, until all the votes [were counted].
And so the name came to my heart: Francis of Assisi. For me he
is the man of poverty, the man of peace, the man who love and
safeguards Creation. In this moment when our relationship with
Creation is not so good—right?—He is the man who gives us this
spirit of peace, the poor man … Oh, how I wish for a Church that
is poor and for the poor! (Catholic News, 2013, para 7).

2   Cox, 2013.
3   Gutiérrez, 1991, p. 181.
4   It is no secret that under the papacy of John Paul II, with Cardinal Joseph
Ratzinger (later Pope Benedict XVI) as prefect of the Congregation of
the Doctrine of the Faith, Gutiérrez's work had been marginalized and
even misunderstood by the Vatican, and though not officially silenced,
he was not fully embraced. While it is beyond the scope for discussion
here, in brief, a central controversial issue with liberation theology is that,
as pointed out by the late Dominican Friar and Latin American scholar
Edward L. Cleary (1985), it borrows parts of a Marxist analysis to explain
economic and social conditions. Yet, as Cleary further explains, echoing
the writings of Gutiérrez, borrowing insight from Marx does not make
one a Marxist; even non-Marxist sociologists acknowledge that Karl Marx
made a significant contribution to social analysis in his calling attention
to class as an element in social life, as both American sociologists and
social journalists have conducted many studies based on class. Moreover,
as the late Henri Nouwen, the Dutch Catholic priest who has written
extensively on Catholic spirituality, writes in the Foreword to Gustavo
Gutiérrez's book *We Drink from Our Own Wells* (1984), "Gustavo begins
his book with the words: 'A Christian is defined as a follower of Jesus,'
and he dedicates the core chapter of this work to an exploration of those
opening words. Those who do not grasp the centrality of Jesus in the
struggle for full human freedom will always misinterpret liberation
theology as well as liberation spirituality … Those who see in liberation
theology a theological rationale for a class struggle in which the poor
claim their rights and try to break the power of their oppressors have
ignored the center of the struggle for freedom. Jesus is the center"
(p. xvii). Finally, particularly pleasing to Gustavo Gutiérrez and others, a
1986 document, *Instruction on Christian Freedom and Liberation*, by the

Sacred Congregation for the Doctrine of the Faith, asserted that liberation
is an important concept in Christian theology, acknowledging the need to
change unjust structures in society (Cox, 1988; McGovern, 1989).

5   San Martín, 2015, para. 2. Pope Francis commenced that change in
atmosphere right from the start of his pontificate. In his first appearance
to the world standing at the central balcony of St. Peter's, Francis did
away with the gaudy Papal cape as part of his dress, simply keeping with
the white traditional vestments, adorned with the same cross he had
always worn as both bishop and cardinal (Boff, 2014). Speaking to the
people for the first time as pope, Francis in quick order asked the throngs
to say the "Lord's Prayer" in unison, later humbly asking the crowd to
pray for him. Moreover, instead of living in the Papal apartments in the
Apostolic Palace, he opted to live in the Vatican guesthouse, enjoying
the company of the community of bishops, priests, and visiting guests.
These early decisions—simple but symbolically impactful—have come
as no surprise to those who knew Jorge Mario Bergoglio; as bishop in
Buenos Aires he lived in a small apartment, cooked for himself, and took
public transportation. Later, in Pope Francis' first trip outside of Rome,
he sojourned to Lampedusa (a Mediterranean island) to greet and bring
comfort to weary, hungry, and tired refugees making the treacherous
journey from Africa who aimed to make their way to Europe for a better
life (Cox, 2013). The release of his first Apostolic Exhortation, *Evangelii
Gaudium* (The Joy of the Gospel), in November 2013 drew from the
Vatican II document (*Gaudium et Spes*), which underscored an emphasis
on a care for the poor. In other words, in *Evangelii Gaudium*, Pope Francis
not only revived the spirit and language of *Gaudium et Spes*, but the
message of Medellín was also revived (Cox, 2013, para 5). Finally, as only
one more example in which Pope Francis has been blowing a wind of a
changed atmosphere in the Church, he took a week-long, three-country
trip to the South American Continent in July 2015. He first stopped in
Ecuador where an admirer, Filiberto Rojos, fervently proclaimed, "We
haven't had a pope like this in a long time, a humble pope, a pope of the
poor, a pope of the people," and where in turn the Pontiff announced that
we must extend "special attention to our most fragile brothers and the
most vulnerable minorities, the debt that is still owed by Latin America"
(Neuman, 2015, para 5, 17). Later in Bolivia, as mentioned, he offered

an apology on behalf of the Church for its exploitive role in colonialism (Yardley & Neuman, 2015). The final leg of his trip took him to Paraguay, and while in the capital city of Asunción, he particularly wanted to visit the banks of the Rio Paraguay to Norte Bañado, one of the poorest areas in the city. Constantly under the threat of being flooded, where shanty homes are made even worse by the elements, and where economic deprivation is common place, Pope Francis shared with the people of Norte Bañado, "I have looked forward to being with you here today … I could not come to Paraguay without spending some time with you, here on your land" (de Diego, Flores & Burke, 2015, para 2).

6   Yardley & Neuman, 2015.

7   Brown, 1980; Batstone, 1991.

8   Los textos de medellín y el proceso de cambio en America Latina, primera edición. (1977). (M. Hernandez-Lehmann, Trans.). San Salvador Centroamerica: UCA/Editores.

9   Lernoux, 1980.

10 Dorrien, 1990, p. 101. Also, to be sure, liberation theology is not just restricted to a Latin American reality. Wherever oppressive forces are at work, the possibility of liberation theology exists (e.g., Palestinian theology of liberation, Black theology of liberation, feminist theology of liberation, among others).

11 Brown, 1990; Gutiérrez, 2013; Gutiérrez, 2015. It must be noted that particularly following Vatican II and the Medellín and Puebla Conferences and its impact on the shaping of liberation theology thinking, many clergy and those in the laity were deeply led to work with and for the poor and marginalized in an effort to empower them as social and political agents of change. These efforts did not come without a great price as the establishment was greatly threatened with the undoing of the status quo, leading to the persecution to both the laity and clergy who were arrested, kidnapped, tortured, raped, exiled, and killed (Lernoux, 1980).

12 Gutiérrez, 1984; Gutiérrez, 1990.

13 Because of his ardent activism, Câmara was subjected to a wave of interrogations and death threats, yet he refused personal protection citing the Father, Son, and Holy Spirit as his shelter (Lalli, 1999; Rocha, 2009). While he was characterized as "the red bishop," Câmara was unwavering in the assertion that he was not a subversive, a Marxist, or a communist,

simply declaring the establishment's contradiction and manipulation, famously asserting, "I feed the poor, I'm called a saint. I ask why the poor have no food, I'm called a communist" (Lalli, 1999, para. 3). The Vatican granted authorization to initiate Câmara's cause for canonization in 2015.

14 Lovett, 2020.

15 To expound further, Gustavo Gutiérrez shares that the translation of the word "option" from the Spanish to the English is problematic, making it the "weakest" word in the phrase, further elaborating,

> In English, the word merely connotes a choice between two things. In Spanish, however, it evokes the sense of commitment. The option for the poor is not optional, but is incumbent upon every Christian. It is not something that a Christian can either take or leave … The option for the poor is twofold: it involves standing in solidarity *with* the poor, but it also entails a stance *against* inhumane poverty (Gutiérrez, 2003, para. 10–11).

16 Gutiérrez, 1987.

17 Brown, 1993.

18 Ibid., pp. 31–2.

19 National Conference of Catholic Bishops, 1986, pp. vii–viii.

Chapter 8

1 Freire, 1985; Freire, 1994; Freire, 1998b; Freire & Vittoria, 2007.

2 Schubeck, 1993, p. 51.

3 Gutiérrez, 1984; Gutiérrez, 1990.

4 Cox, 1988, p. 183.

5 Gutiérrez, 1973, p. 24.

6 Freire, 1985.

7 Gutiérrez, 1973; Gutiérrez, 1990.

8 Romero, 1978, p. 62.

9 Bonhoeffer, 1963.

10 Mcdonagh, 1987.

11 Whether it is Maximilian Kolbe, Joan of Arc, Medgar Evers, Dietrich Bonhoeffer, or the numerous first responders that went up the twin towers on 9/11, there are many known and unknown cases in which

courageous individuals have given up their lives up for the other.
And while the ultimate sacrifice of laying down one's life is death is
martyrdom, it is also true that daily—whether one is a person of faith
or not—we each have opportunities to lay down our lives in the way we
extend a helping hand to a child in need; in the way we take the coat off
our back and give it to a brother; in the way we offer a cup of water to a
sister; and in the way we offer our time, talent, abilities, and resources to
those in need.

12 Lewis, 1960.
13 King, 1967, p. 42.
14 Lewis, 2020, p. 13.
15 Ave Maria Press, 2015.

Chapter 9

1 Pinar & Grumet, 1976; Pinar, 1994; Pinar, Reynolds, Slattery & Taubman, 1995; Slattery, 1995.
2 Ibid.
3 Ibid.
4 Giroux, 1988.
5 Koch, 2009.
6 Kirylo, 2011.
7 Giroux, 2020, p. 2.
8 Pinar, Reynolds, Slattery & Taubman, 1995.
9 Milani, 1957, p. 203.
10 Nouwen, 1983, p. 118.
11 To be sure, a conversation about poverty and education is multifaceted, intersecting the social sciences, politics, economics, religious, and theological persuasions, and questions of race, gender, and culture. Moreover, a conversation about poverty and solutions to its challenges can be very different between "developed" and "developing" countries. While I have lived in Europe, South America, and currently live in the United States, and while perhaps some of my perspectives here can be generalized, others obviously may not, simply dictated by the multidimensional happenings of a respective country.

12 Grimes, 1996.

13 Rose, 1995, p. 2.

14 Gutiérrez, 1996.

15 Moore, Redd, Burkhauser, Mbwana & Collins, 2009.

16 There is no doubt regarding the effect of poverty on young people, with implications that are varied, multifaceted, and complex. This is not to disregard, however, that despite the impact of poverty, many young people heroically and resiliently rise above their circumstances through the combinational efforts of wide-ranging support systems such as good parenting and encouraging family structures; through the support of the faith community; through the support of mentors; through the support of governmental intervention; through the support of good schools; through the support of quality after-school programs; and, a host of other entities. While it takes a family to raise a child, it also takes a village to pave the road in order to facilitate a child's growth.

17 In order to guide students to make conceptual connections between what they know and what they need to learn, the teacher, in these instances, acts more like a facilitator, realizing that students may be in need of "scaffolding" (i.e., guidance, support). A concept developed by Vygotsky, scaffolding can occur through a teacher, peer, parent, etc., where the student is working within a zone of proximal development. That zone is the place where the student is able or is capable of doing a task, but with assistance (scaffolding) in order to reach that place of learning (Vygotsky, 1978; Slavin, 2000).

18 For more detail on this point, please see my work Kirylo, 2021.

19 Catechism of the Catholic church, 1997, p. 465, nos. 1907–1910.

20 Pontifical Council for Justice and Peace (2004), p. 73, No. 165.

21 Kirylo & Boyd, 2017.

22 There is, of course, a necessary conversation to be had between the place of personal responsibility and the intervention role of government or any other social services. Systemic and generational poverty, however, has nothing to do with lack of responsibility, motivation, or desire; rather, the problem is lack of opportunity, poor wages, and a host of other interrelated dynamics that have created the conditions in which the poor find themselves, which is on the outside looking in. See the parable of the rich man and Lazarus (Lk. 16: 19-31).

23 Barshad, 2020; Perrigo, 2020.
24 Perrigo, 2020.
25 Barshad, 2020, para. 5.
26 Perrigo, 2020, para. 3.
27 Pope John Paul II, 1987.

Chapter 10

1 Rohr, 2019, p. 94.
2 Banks, 2017, p. xii. As the series editor for his Multicultural Education Series, Banks echoes Sensoy and DiAngelo in the aforementioned book.
3 1 Pet. 3:15-16.
4 Sensoy & DiAngelo, 2017, p. 29.

Chapter 11

1 Centers for Disease Control and Prevention, n.d.
2 Center for Disease Philanthropy (CDP), n.d.
3 Sanger, Lipton, Sullivan & Crowley, 2020.
4 McElwee, 2021.
5 With the assumption that one is informed by thoughtful, relevant, and legitimate information to inform religious, moral, ethical, or medical reasons for not taking the vaccine, no one should be "forced" to be injected. Yet, if that be the case one should be subjected to precautions, such as regular testing and mask-wearing.
6 NPR, 2021, para. 3–4.
7 Sandel, 2020
8 O'Grady, 2022.
9 Nogrady, 2021.
10 Mt. 12:25.
11 Franciscan Sisters of Perpetual Adoration, n.d.

Chapter 12

1   Gun Violence Archive, n.d.

2   For an individual to own a firearm in Italy, one must be minimally
     eighteen years of age to apply for a license. Moreover, one must not have
     a criminal record and must obtain a signed certificate from a physician
     that there is no addiction to drugs or mental health concerns; the same
     criteria also apply when one inherits a firearm or is received as a gift.
     And within seventy-two hours of owning a firearm, the weapon must be
     registered with the local police station. Upon selling or giving a firearm
     to another person, local authorities must be notified. Upon leaving the
     home with a firearm, gun owners must have a hunting or sporting license
     on hand, suggesting that the only reason the firearm is on hand (i.e., on
     person or in vehicle) is to participate in respective hunting or sporting
     activities. Concealed weapon permits are only administered if one can
     present documentation that she or he is in a line of work where personal
     safety is of concern, a license which needs to be annually renewed. And
     upon ownership of a firearm, if there is evidence of changed behavior
     (e.g., violence, threatening behavior, mental instability), the firearm can
     be seized by local authorities. After a period of time, the firearm can be
     reclaimed upon a doctor's certification that the individual is more stable.
     Finally, while Italy allows for handguns, hunting rifles, shotguns, sports
     shooting guns, antique or historical firearms, low-muzzle energy airguns,
     fully automatic and semi-automatic assault-type weapons, military or
     police-grade weapons, and noise suppressors or silencers are illegal
     (Heath, 2021).

3   Charles, n.d.; Shusterman, 2018; The Editors of Encyclopaedia, n.d.

4   Ibid.

5   It is important to note that when the Second Amendment was ratified,
     the idea of a citizenry militia was also used as a means to police (and/
     or suppress) Blacks and native populations, meaning their right to bear
     arms was not inclusive in the Amendment. And to the present day, when
     it comes to the Second Amendment, the racist legacy of the United
     States continues to manifest its ugly head, as historian Carol Anderson
     asserts, "When I looked at the individual right to bear arms, when I
     looked at the right to a well-regulated militia, and when I looked at the

right to self-defense all over time, I'm seeing that those do not apply to Black Americans—in fact, each of those have been used *against* African Americans because it is the quality of anti-Blackness, to define African Americans as a threat, as dangerous, as criminal, as people who need to be subjugated and controlled. Even if you are unarmed, you're still a threat. How many times have we in this current day heard of a Black person being gunned down simply because they had a cellphone and somebody felt threatened because they thought it was a gun? … It doesn't matter whether you have a gun or don't. Your Blackness is the threat, and it is the default threat in this society" (Anderson, 2021, para 15–16).

6   Charles, n.d.; History.com Editors, n.d.; Shusterman, 2018.

7   In the United States, under federal law, one has to be at least twenty-one years old to purchase a handgun, and eighteen years of age to purchase a long gun (e.g., rifle or shotgun). And while the federal government imposed an assault weapon ban from 1994 to 2004—a ban supported by the United States Conference of Catholic Bishops—the Assault Weapons Ban was not renewed. Hence, as of this writing, there is no federal legislation regarding the purchasing of military style assault weapons, meaning that in most states the minimal age is eighteen years of age for that type of transaction. Federal law requires background checks when an individual purchases a firearm from a licensed dealer; yet, this comes with a "loophole" in which anyone can purchase a weapon of choice from an unlicensed dealer, friends, or relatives without a background check. And despite historical precedent that ardently prohibited or regulated open carry (the carrying of firearms in public), it has now become quite common in a variety of states where restrictions are quite lax. As it currently stands, over forty states in the United States allow open carry without a permit, including loaded semi-automatic rifles (see: https://www.everytown.org/; https://giffords.org/lawcenter/gun-laws/).

8   On average, 36,000 Americans are killed by firearms every year (gun suicides: 22,274 (61 percent); gun homicides: 12,830 (35 percent); law enforcement shootings: 496 (1.4 percent); unintentional shootings: 487 (1.3 percent); undetermined: 295 (0.8 percent), with another approximately 100,000 who are annually wounded by them. For the latter, this averages out to 284 gunshot injuries per day, and for the former the average is 100 deaths per day (Gun Violence Statistics, n.d.).

9   Allen, 2019.

10 Graf, 2018.

11 Schmelzer, 2019.

12 This statement was made by then–NRA executive vice president, Wayne LaPierre, in response to the 2012 Sandy Hook Elementary School Shooting in Newton, Connecticut, where 20 six- and seven-year-old children and six educators were murdered by a domestic terrorist using assault-style weaponry. And while that statement was asserted years ago, the sentiment largely remains the rallying call of the gun community (Overby, 2012).

13 Nogales, 2018.

14 Lee, 2019.

15 United States Conference of Catholic Bishops, 2020.

16 Ibid.

17 Everytown for Gun Safety, n.d.

18 Giffords Law Center to Prevent Gun Violence, n.d.

19 Gun Violence Archive, n.d.

20 Kerr, 2022.

21 Miami Herald Editorial Board, 2022.

Chapter 13

1   The Catechism of the Catholic Church (1997) explains it this way: "Human life must be respected and protected absolutely from the moment of conception. From the first moment of his existence, a human being must be recognized as having the rights of a person—among which is the inviolable right of every innocent being to life … Since the first century the Church has affirmed the moral evil of every procured abortion. This teaching has not changed and remains unchangeable" pp. 547–8 (2270-2271). See also Jer. 1:15, Job 10:8-12, Ps. 22:10-11, Ps. 139: 15, and Isa. 44:24.

2   In other words, "From the time that the ovum is fertilized, a life is begun which is neither that of the father nor of the mother, it is rather the life of a new human being with his own growth. It would never be made human if it were not human already" (Sacred Congregation for the Doctrine of the Faith in its Declaration on Procured Abortion, 1974, para. 12).

3 Chertoff, 2018. The "leap in the womb" reference is taken from the Lucan passage when Mary, pregnant with Jesus, visited her cousin Elizabeth, who was pregnant with John (the Baptist), and "When Elizabeth heard Mary's greetings, the infant leaped in her womb, and Elizabeth, filled with the holy Spirit, cried out in a loud voice and said, "Most blessed are you among women, and blessed is the fruit of your womb" (Lk. 1:41-42).

4 Aristotle, 1932; Lu, 2013; Brady, 2020.

5 Silber, 1980; Schenker, 2008.

6 Feldman, 1968, p. 257.

7 Silber, 1980.

8 Brady, 2020.

9 Ibid.

10 Percy, n.d.

11 Such as adoption, as underscored in the epigraph, Mother Teresa, 1994, para. 6.

12 Carter, 1991, p. 2764.

13 Pope John Paul II, 1995.

14 It is from the Jesuit Father James Martin (2019) that I derived this particular thought when he states in a compelling piece titled, "Why I am pro-life": "But acknowledging that women's bodies are their own does not diminish my own reverence for the living body in a woman's womb" (para. 14).

15 Rohr, 2013, p. 2.

Chapter 14

1 Praying Nature with St. Francis of Assisi, n.d.

2 For example, see Genesis 1:1-31; Genesis 2:15; Leviticus 25: 1-7; Deuteronomy 10:14; Psalm 24:1-2; Daniel 3:56-82; Matthew 6:25-34; Romans 1:20; I Corinthians 10:26.

3 History.com Editors (2019, 2009); Industrial revolution, 2021.

4 Ibid.

5 Nunez, 2019.

6 Ibid.; Rafferty, n.d.

7 Nunez, 2019.

8   EPA, n.d.; Konyn, 2021.
9   Carbon Neutrality Initiative, n.d.; Climatetrade, n.d.
10 Denchak, 2016; MacMillan & Turrentine, 2021.
11 Pope Francis, 2015, pp. 21–2.
12 NASA, n.d.
13 Patriarch Bartholomew, 2015, p. 11.
14 Pope John Paul II, 2001.
15 Deaton & Jenkins, 2016.
16 Denchak, 2021.
17 Pope Francis, 2020c; Maizland, 2021.
18 Pope Benedict VI, 2011, para. 10.
19 Maizland, 2021.
20 For example, see: https://www.usccb.org/resources/why-does-church-care-about-global-climate-change.
21 Pope Benedict, 2010, para. 4–5.

Chapter 15

1   Sacrament, n.d.
2   Augustine, n.d., c, para 3.
3   Moore, 2004; Groome, 2019.
4   Mother Teresa, 1996, p. 9.
5   Chambers, 1935, p. 241.
6   See, for example, 2 Chron. 16:9; Ps. 18:26-27; Jas 3:17-18.
7   Rohr, 1999, p. 70.
8   McNeill, Morrison & Nouwen, 1982.
9   Mt. 23: 1-39; Mk 7:1-23.
10 Merton, 1961, p. 196.
11 While the monastery was a welcomed area presence for seventy years, it was forced to shut its doors in 2017 because of a combination of aging monks and dwindling numbers of novitiates.
12 As a point of clarification, while the concepts of contemplation and meditation are often used interchangeably, they are technically different. For the latter, as pointed out in the Catechism of the Catholic Church (1997), "Meditation is above all a quest. The mind seeks to understand

the why and how of the Christian life, in order to adhere and respond to what the Lord is asking…To meditate on what we read helps us to make it our own by confronting it with ourselves…Meditation engages thought, imagination, emotion, and desire" (pp. 649–50). For the former, again, according to the Catechism of the Catholic Church, "Contemplative prayer is the simple expression of the mystery of prayer. It is a gaze of faith fixed on Jesus, an attentiveness to the Word of God, a silent love. It achieves real union with the prayer of Christ to the extent that it makes us share in his mystery" (p. 653).

13 Nouwen, 1979, p. 103.
14 Keating, 1997, p. 146.
15 Merton, 1987, p. 50, 110.
16 Keating, 1997.
17 Merton, 1961, p. 111.
18 Julian of Norwich (n.d.). *Revelations of Divine Love*. (Trans: G. Warrack). Christian Classics Ethereal Library. The full translation also reads like the following: "God, of Thy Goodness, give me Thyself: for Thou art enough to me, and I may nothing ask that is less that may be full worship to Thee; and if I ask anything that is less, ever me wanteth,—but only in Thee I have all" (p. 11). Retrieved on 2/24/2022 from https://ccel.org/ccel/j/julian/revelations/cache/revelations.pdf.
19 Rohr, 2020, para. 1.
20 In his book, *God's Politics: Why the Right Gets It Wrong and the Left Doesn't Get*, Jim Wallis (2005) explains it this way: "God is personal, but never private…Private religion avoids the public consequences of faith" (p. 31).
21 Dulles, 1977.
22 Gutiérrez, 1984; Gutiérrez, 1990.
23 Rohr, 1987b.

Afterword

1 Goodlad, Soder & Sirotnik, 1990.
2 Schuttloffel, 1999, 2008, 2019.
3 Schuttloffel, 2008.

Appendix A

1   Tanner, 2011; Weidenkopf, 2018.
2   When the Nicene Creed was translated into Latin, the translation read
    that the Holy Spirit proceeded from the "Father and the Son," as was
    favored by the Western Church, as opposed to the original Greek, which
    was favored by the Eastern Church, which read "And in the Holy Spirit,
    the Lord and Giver of life, who proceeds from the Father, who together
    with the Father and the Son is worshipped and glorified." It was during
    the 589 Council of Toledo, Spain, in which the *filioque* clause first
    appeared in Latin (Saunders, n.d.).
3   Tanner, 2011; Weidenkopf, 2018.
4   Pope Paul VI, & Patriarch Athenagoras I (1965), para. 4B.
5   Saunders, n.d.
6   According to the Catholic Church, the doctrine of Purgatory is grounded
    in the scriptures and ecclesiastically emerged in 1274 at the Second
    Council in Lyon. As such Purgatory is "A state of final purification after
    death and before entrance into heaven for those who died in God's
    friendship, but were only imperfectly purified; a final cleansing of human
    imperfection before one is able to enter the joy heaven" (Catechism of the
    Catholic Church, 1997, p. 896). While the origin of indulgences appears
    to have unfolded in the early centuries of the persecuted church, it was
    in the eleventh century that indulgences became notably pronounced
    under papal authority as an incentive to join the Crusades. Moreover, in
    light of the Black (Bubonic) Plague in the fourteenth century, the notion
    of indulgences became even more heightened as there was an acute
    preoccupation of death and the afterlife (O'Malley, 2009; MacCulloch,
    2010; Zentner, 2015).
7   See ninety-five theses here: https://www.luther.de/en/95thesen.html.
8   The germination of the Protestant Reformation was in motion prior to
    the posting of the ninety-five theses, with the work of Jan (or John) Huss
    (1369–1415) and John Wycliffe (1328–84), to name only two. And still
    others followed Martin Luther in moving forward with the Reformation,
    notably Ulrich Zwingli (1484–1531) and John Calvin (1509–64), among
    others. As the Protestant Reformation unfolded and as a result of differing

theological viewpoints, they subdivided into various groups, leading into multiple Protestant dominations (e.g., Lutherans, Baptists, Methodists, Presbyterians) and nondenominational groups (e.g., Hillsong Church, Vineyard Church, The Potter's House). All told, and depending on the source, there are figures that state there are 47,000, to 33,000, to 188 Protestant denominations, with an estimated 35,000 nondenominational churches (Beale, 2017).

9   Bokenkotter, 2005, p. 242.

10 Ibid.; Duggan, 2015.

11 Christianity is the world's largest religion, comprised of approximately 31 percent of the 7.3 billion people living on earth. Of that percentage, 50.1 percent are Catholic, 36.7 percent are Protestant, 11.9 percent are Orthodox, and 1.3 percent other Christian (Hackett & McClendon, 2017; Sahgal, 2017).

Appendix B

1   Parts of Appendices B and C are adapted from my work, *Paulo Freire: His Faith, Spirituality, and Theology* (with Drick Boyd) (2017, Sense).

2   While the ancient Hebrews were naturally conscious of the notion of human virtues, there was no term in the Hebrew Scriptures (Old Testament) that intimated a conventional meaning of virtue. However, when the Old Testament was translated from the Hebrew to the Greek (Septuagint), the word *arête* (virtue or excellence) surfaces (see, for example, Wis 4:1 and 5:13). While in the Christian Scriptures (New Testament) the word "virtue" is not often used—perhaps because of the anthropocentric (a central focus on a human driven initiative as opposed to spiritually driven) nature of the word—it was a term that was referred to when it came to moral goodness (see, for example, Phil. 4:8; 1 Pet. 2:9; 2 Pet. 1:3, 1:5). It is also true, however, that in the early Christian community, especially expressed in the Pauline letters, the notion of virtues was linked to spirituality and not due to human doing, especially when it came to the virtues of faith and love, ultimately the transforming agent of all other virtues (Walter, 1987).

3   Walter, 1987; Richert, 2019.

4 Walter, 1987.
5 Aquinas, 1981, p. 851.
6 Dulles, 1977.
7 Komonchak, Collins & Lane, 1987, p. 493.
8 Augustine (n.d., a). *Homilies on the first epistle of John* (Homily 7) (1 Jn 4:4-12). (para. 8). *New Advent*. Retrieved on 5/14/2021 from https://www.newadvent.org/fathers/170207.htm. Augustine (n.d., b) also memorably declared, "You have formed us for Yourself, and our hearts are restless till they find rest in You" (para 1). Living a life of excess, attempting to embrace a variety of philosophies of life, and continually searching for meaning, Augustine eventually came to that place of personal transformation in which his peace and meaning in life rested in his love for the living Christ.

Appendix C

1 Richert, 2019.
2 Ibid.
3 Walter, 1987.

References

Al Jazeera (2021, Aug. 18). More than 1,000 killed in Myanmar since February 1 coup. Retrieved on 1/20/2022 from https://www.aljazeera.com/news/2021/8/18/myanmar-coup-aapp-1000-killed-military.

Allen, J.R. (2019, Aug. 5). Gun violence in America: A true national security threat. Retrieved on 10/04/2021 from https://www.brookings.edu/blog/brookings-now/2019/08/05/gun-violence-in-america-a-true-national-security-threat/.

Al-Marashi, I. (2021, Mar. 9). Pope Francis's visit to Iraq: Beyond the symbolism. *Al Jazeera Media Network*. Retrieved on 3/13/2021 from https://www.aljazeera.com/opinions/2021/3/9/pope-franciss-visit-to-iraq-beyond-the-symbolism.

Amin, R. (2019, Jan. 13). Importance of interfaith dialogue. *Bozeman Daily Chronicle*. Retrieved on 12/23/2021 from https://www.bozemandailychronicle.com/religion/importance-of-interfaith-dialogue/article_4b3f5a24-9eb4-59a7-b12d-d4c85d2bd522.html.

Anderson, C. (2021, Aug. 3). In D. Lithwick, "The second amendment is not intended for Black people:" Tracing the racist history of gun governance. *Slate*. Retrieved on 9/20/2021 from https://slate.com/news-and-politics/2021/08/second-amendment-guns-racist-black-americans-history.html.

Andrés, J. (2019, Sept. 4). In A. Greely, Meet José Andrés, famous chef & Catholic humanitarian (para. 6). *Catholic Exchange*. Retrieved on 1/19/2022 from https://catholicexchange.com/jose-andres-famous-chef-catholic-humanitarian/.

Apostolicam Actuositatem (1965, Nov. 18). Decree on the apostolate of the laity apostolicam actuositatem. Solemnly promulgated by his holiness Pope Paul VI. *The Holy See*. Retrieved on 3/20/2021 from http://www.vatican.va/archive/hist_councils/ii_vatican_council/documents/vat-ii_decree_19651118_apostolicam-actuositatem_en.html.

Aquinas, T. (1981). *Summa theologica* (V. 2) (Translated by Fathers of the English Dominican Province) (p. 851). Allen, TX: Christian Classics: A Division of Thomas More Publishing (originally published in English in 1911—copyright 1948 by Benziger Brothers, Inc., NY).

Archdiocese of Chicago (n.d.). *Office for Ecumenical and Interreligious Affairs.* Retrieved on 3/8/2021 from http://legacy.archchicago.org/departments/ ecumenical/relations.htm.

Aristotle (1932). *Politics* (Translated by H. Rackham). Cambridge, MA: Harvard University Press.

Arthur, J.F. (2015, Jun. 23). *The call to teach: Expectations for the Catholic educator in magisterial teaching.* Manassas, VA: The Cardinal Newman Society. Retrieved on 3/28/2021 from https://newmansociety.org/call-teach-expectations-catholic-educator-magisterial-teaching/.

Augustine (n.d., a). Homilies on the first epistle of John (Homily 7) (1 John 4:4-12). *New Advent.* Retrieved on 5/14/2021 from https://www. newadvent.org/fathers/170207.htm.

Augustine (n.d., b). He proclaims the greatness of God, whom he desires to seek and invoke, being awakened by Him (Chapter 1). The Confessions (Book 1). *New Advent.* Retrieved on 5/14/2021 from https://www. newadvent.org/fathers/110101.htm.

Augustine (n.d., c). In J.E. Oliver (2020, May 15). Sacrament. *Encyclopedia Britannica.* Retrieved on 1/27/2022 from https://www.britannica.com/ topic/sacrament.

Ave Maria Press (2015). *Foundations of Catholic social teaching: Living as a disciple of Christ.* Notre Dame, IN: Ave Maria Press.

Banks, J.A. (2017). In Ö. Sensoy, & R. DiAngelo, *Is everyone really equal: An introduction to key concepts in social justice education* (2nd edition). New York: Teachers College Press.

Barshad, A. (2020, Nov. 30). After growing up poor, as a Premier League star corners U.K. into feeding its hungry. *The Washington Post.* Retrieved on 7/20/2021 from https://www.washingtonpost.com/sports/2020/11/30/ marcus-rashford-uk-hunger/.

Batstone, D. (1991). *From conquest to struggle: Jesus of Nazareth in Latin America.* New York: State University of New York Press.

Beale, S. (2017, Oct. 31). Just how many Protestant denominations are there? *National Catholic Register.* Retrieved on 3/8/2021 from https://www. ncregister.com/blog/just-how-many-protestant-%09denominations-are-therehttps://www.ncregister.com/blog/just-how-many-protestant-denominations-are-there.

Berryman, P. (1987). *Liberation theology: Essential facts about the revolutionary movement in Latin America and beyond.* Philadelphia, PA: Temple University Press.

Boff, L. (2014). *Francis of Rome and Francis of Assisi: A new springtime for the church*. Maryknoll, NY: Orbis Books.

Bokenkotter, T. (2005). *A concise history of the Catholic church* (Revised and expanded edition). New York: Image Books, Doubleday.

Bonhoeffer, D. (1963). *The cost of discipleship*. New York: Macmillan.

Bowling, M. (2021, Mar. 26). Amidst escalating violence, a solitary nun stands her ground. *The Catholic Leader*. Retrieved on 1/19/2022 from https://catholicleader.com.au/news/amidst-escalating-violence-a-solitary-nun-stands-her-ground/.

Bowman, T. (2015). Sr. Thea Bowman, FSPA: What does it mean to be Black and Catholic? Retrieved on 1/22/2022 from https://www.youtube.com/watch?v=d6pBrBOawII.

Brady, M. (2020). Roman Catholic church teaching and abortion: A historical view from the early church to modern day. [Unpublished thesis]. Baylor University.

Britannica, T. Editors of Encyclopaedia (2021, Jul. 21). Industrial Revolution. *Encyclopedia Britannica*. Retrieved on 11/24/2021 from https://www.britannica.com/event/Industrial-Revolution.

Brockman, J.R. (1989). *Romero: A life*. Maryknoll, NY: Orbis Books.

Brown, R.M. (1980). *Gustavo Gutiérrez* (p. 13). Atlanta, GA: John Knox Press.

Brown, R.M. (1990). *Gustavo Gutiérrez: An introduction to liberation theology*. Maryknoll, NY: Orbis Books.

Brown, R.M. (1993). *Liberation theology: An introductory guide*. Louisville, KY: Westminster/John Knox Press.

Buber, M. (1958). *I and thou* (2nd edition). New York, NY: Scribner.

Buck, P. (1950). Before the AASA Convention, Atlantic City. In W.A. Jenkins, "The educational scene." *Elementary English*, *27*(5), pp. 339–43. Retrieved on 12/28/2021 from http://www.jstor.org/stable/41383750.

Burford, T.O. (n.d.). Personalism. *Internet Encyclopedia of Philosophy: A Peer-reviewed Academic Resource*. Retrieved on 04/16/2021 from https://iep.utm.edu/personal/.

Carbon Neutrality Initiative (n.d.). Where do greenhouse gas emissions come from? *University of California*. Retrieved on 11/30/2021 from https://www.universityofcalifornia.edu/longform/where-do-greenhouse-gas-emissions-come.

Carter, S.L. (1991). Abortion, absolutism, and compromise [Review of the book *Abortion: The clash of absolutes*, by L.H. Tribe]. *The Yale Law Journal*, *100*(8), pp. 2747–66.

Catechism of the Catholic Church (1997). *Revised in accordance with the official Latin text promulgated by Pope John Paul II* (2nd edition). Citta del Vaticano: Libreria Editrice Vaticana.

Catholic News (2013, Mar. 16). *Pope Francis: "Oh, how i wish for a church that is poor and for the poor!"* Retrieved on 6/3/2021 from https://catholicnews. sg/2013/03/18/pope-francis-oh-how-i-wish-for-a-church-that-is-poor-and-for-the-poor/.

Center for Disease Philanthropy (CDP) (n.d.). COVID-19 coronavirus. Retrieved on 5/12/2022 from https://disasterphilanthropy.org/disasters/ covid-19-coronavirus/?gclid=EAIaIQobChMIiq7qxqra9wIVsdGCh0xVQa UEAAYAyAAEgJn6PD_BwE.

Centers for Disease Control and Prevention (n.d.). *Basics of Covid-19.* Retrieved on 8/18/2021 from https://www.cdc.gov/coronavirus/2019-ncov/your-health/about-covid-19/basics-covid-19.html.

Chambers, O. (1935). *My utmost for his highest.* Westwood, NJ: Barbour and Company, Inc.

Chandler, C.K., Holden, J.M., & Kolander, C.A. (1992). Counseling for spiritual wellness: Theory and practice. *Journal of Counseling and Development, 71*(2), pp. 168–75.

Charles, P.J. (n.d.). Second amendment. *Encyclopedia Britannica.* Retrieved on 9/17/2021 from https://www.britannica.com/topic/Second-Amendment.

Chertoff, J. (2018, Sept. 26). How early can you hear baby's heartbeat on ultrasound and by ear? Medically reviewed by V.R. Nwadike, MD, MPH. *Healthline.* Retrieved on 11/12/201 from https://www.healthline.com/ health/pregnancy/when-can-you-hear-babys-heartbeat.

Chittister, J. (2010). *The rule of Benedict: A spirituality for the 21ˢᵗ century.* New York: Crossroad.

Chryssavgis, J. (2014, May 23–27). Pilgrimage toward unity: Ecumenical Patriarch Athenagoras and Pope Paul in Jerusalem (1964) based on correspondence and archives. Apostolic Pilgrimage to Jerusalem. Retrieved on 3/12/2021 from https://www.apostolicpilgrimage.org/historicmeeting.

Cleary, E.L. (1985). *Crises and change: The church in Latin America today.* Maryknoll, NY: Orbis Books.

Climatetrade (n.d.). Which countries are the world's biggest carbon polluters? Retrieved on 11/30/2021 from https://climatetrade.com/which-countries-are-the-worlds-biggest-carbon-polluters/.

Cogley, J. (2020, Nov. 21). *Saint John XXIII. Encyclopedia Britannica.* Retrieved on 3/16/2021 from https://www.britannica.com/biography/Saint-John-XXIII.

Cox, H. (1988). *The silencing of Leonardo Boff.* Oak Park, IL: Meyer–Stone Books.

Cox, H. (2013, Dec. 18). Is Pope Francis the new champion of liberation theology? *The Nation.* Retrieved on 6/3/2021 from http://www.thenation.com/article/pope-francis-new-champion-liberation-theology/.

Cuddy, A. (2021, Apr. 1). Myanmar coup: What is happening and why? *BBC News.* Retrieved on 1/20/2022 from https://www.bbc.com/news/world-asia-55902070.

Cunningham, L.S. (1987). Humanism. In J.A. Komonchak, M. Collins, & D.A. Lane, *The new dictionary of theology* (pp. 498–500). Collegeville, MN: The Liturgical Press.

Darder, A. (2016, Jan.). Latinos, education, and the church: Toward a culturally democratic future. *Journal of Catholic Education, 19*(2), pp. 18–53.

Das, S. (2015). Significance of Mother Teresa's three stripped sari. *Mother Teresa Center.* Retrieved on 1/13/2022 from https://www.motherteresa.org/08_info/Sari.html.

Day, D. (1945, Sep.). Peter the materialist. *The Catholic Worker.* Retrieved on 4/14/2021 from https://www.catholicworker.org/dorothyday/articles/152.html.

Day, D. (1963, 1997). *Loaves and fishes.* Maryknoll, NY: Orbis Books (Originally published by Harper & Row, 1963).

Deaton, J., & Jenkins, J. (2016, Apr. 18). 250 faith leaders demand nations ratify paris climate deal. *ThinkProgress.* Retrieved on 12/2/2021 from https://archive.thinkprogress.org/250-faith-leaders-demand-nations-ratify-paris-climate-deal-c150f6a30ec3/.

de Cepeda y Ahumada, Teresa (of Avila) (2007). *Interior castle* (The classic text with a spiritual commentary by Dennis Billy, C.Ss.R.). Notre Dame, IN: Ave Maria Press.

de Diego, J., Flores, R., & Burke, D. (2015). *Pope visits slum village in Paraguay.* Retrieved on 6/4/2021 from https://www.cnn.com/2015/07/11/world/pope-francis-paraguay/.

de Las Casas, B. (1974). *The devastation of the Indies: A brief account* (Translated by H. Briffault). Baltimore, MD: The Johns Hopkins University Press.

Denchak, M. (2016, Mar. 15). Are the effects of global warming really that bad? *Natural Resources Defense Council* (NRDC). Retrieved on 11/

30/2021 from https://www.nrdc.org/stories/are-effects-global-warming-really-bad.

Denchak, M. (2021, Feb. 19). Paris climate agreement: Everything you need to know. *Natural Resources Defense Council* (NRDC). Retrieved on 12/2/2021 from https://www.nrdc.org/stories/paris-climate-agreement-everything-you-need-know.

De Tavernier (2009). The historical roots of personalism: From Renouvier's le personnalisme, Mounier's manifeste au service du personnalisme and Maritain's humanisme intégral to Janssens' personne et société. *Ethical Perspectives, 16*(3), pp. 361–92.

Divini Illius, Magistri (1929, Dec. 31). Encyclical of Pope Pius XI on Christian education to the patriarchs, primates, archbishops, bishops, and other ordinaries in peace and communionwith the apostolic see and to all the faithful of the Catholic world. *Libreria Editrice Vaticana*. Retrieved on 3/20/2021 from http://www.vatican.va/content/pius-xi/en/encyclicals/documents/hf_p-xi_enc_31121929_divini-illius-magistri.html.

Donovan, B.M. (1974). Introduction. In B. de Las Casas, *The devastation of the Indies: A brief account* (Translated by H. Briffault) (pp. 1–25). Baltimore, MD: The Johns Hopkins University Press.

Dorr, D. (1983). *Option for the poor: A hundred years of Vatican social teaching.* Maryknoll, NY: Orbis Books.

Dorrien, G.J. (1990). *Reconstructing the common good: Theology and the social order.* Maryknoll, NY: Orbis Books.

Duggan, L.G. (2015, Nov. 25). *Indulgence. Encyclopedia Britannica.* Retrieved 2/1/2021 from https://www.britannica.com/topic/indulgence.

Dulles, A. (1977). The meaning of faith considered in relationship to justice. In *The faith that does justice: Examining the Christian sources for social change* (Edited by S.J. J.C Haughey) (pp. 10–46). New York, NY: Paulist Press.

Dussel, D. (1976). *History and the theology of liberation, a Latin American perspective* (Translated by J. Drury). Maryknoll, NY: Orbis Books.

Dussel, E. (1981). *A history of the church in Latin America: Colonialism to liberation (1492–1979)* (Translated by A. Neely). Grand Rapids, MI: Eerdmans Publishing Company.

The Editors of Encyclopaedia (n.d.). *Encyclopedia Britannica.* Retrieved on 9/17/2021 from https://www.britannica.com/topic/militia.

Edwords, F. (1989, 2008). What is humanism? *American Humanist Association.* Retrieved on 4/17/2021 from https://americanhumanist.org/what-is-humanism/edwords-what-is-humanism/.

Eisenbrandt, M. (2017). *Assassination of a saint: The plot to murder Óscar Romero and the quest to bring his killers to justice.* Oakland, CA: University of California Press.

Ellsberg, R. (2012, Nov. 5). Las Casas' discovery: What the "protector of the Indians" found in America. *America: The Jesuit Review.* Retrieved on 5/27/2021 from https://www.americamagazine.org/issue/las-casas-discovery.

Eneau, J. (2008). From autonomy to reciprocity, or vice versa? French personalism's contribution to a new perspective on self-directed learning. *Adult Education Quarterly, 58*(3), pp. 229–48.

EPA (n.d.). Greenhouse gases. *United States Environmental Protection Agency.* Retrieved on 11/27/2021 from https://www.epa.gov/report-environment/greenhouse-gases.

Everytown for Gun Safety (n.d.). *Prohibit open carry.* Retrieved on 10/12/2021 from https://www.everytown.org/solutions/prohibit-open-carry/.

Everytown for Gun Safety (n.d.). Retrieved on 10/6/2021 from https://www.everytown.org/.

Fedele, A. (2020, Jul. 6). Sister vs. Nun—What's the difference? *African Sisters Education Collaborative (ASEC).* Retrieved on 1/15/2021 from http://asec-sldi.org/news/general/sister-vs-nun/.

Feldman, D.M. (1968). *Birth control in Jewish law.* New York: New York University Press.

Fialka, J.J. (2003). *Sisters: Catholic Nuns and the making of America.* New York: St. Martin's Press.

Franciscan Sisters of Perpetual Adoration (n.d.). *Prayer of St. Francis of Assisi.* Retrieved on 5/11/2022 from https://www.fspa.org/content/prayer/franciscan-prayers.

Fratelli, Tutti (2020, Oct. 3). *Libreria Editrice Vaticana.* Retrieved on 3/16/2021 from http://www.vatican.va/content/francesco/en/encyclicals/documents/papa-francesco_20201003_enciclica-fratelli-tutti.html.

Freire, A. (2011). *An interview with Ana Maria (Nita) Araújo Freire.* In J.D. Kirylo Paulo Freire, The Man from Recife (pp. 271–89). New York, NY: Peter Lang.

Freire, A., & Vittoria, P. (2007, Sept.). Dialogue on Paulo Freire. *Interamerican Journal of Education for Democracy, 1* (1), pp. 97–117. Retrieved from: http://www.ried-ijed.org.

Freire, P. (1985). *The politics of education: Culture, power, and liberation.* New York: Bergin & Garvey.

Freire, P. (1994). *Education for critical consciousness*. New York: Continuum.

Freire, P. (1998a). *Politics and education*. Los Angeles: UCLA Latin American Center Publications.

Freire, P. (1998b). *Pedagogy of freedom: Ethics, democracy, and civic courage*. Lanham, MD: Rowman & Littlefield Publishers, Inc.

Gaudium et Spes (1965). Retrieved on 6/21/2022 from http://www.vatican.va/archive/hist_councils/ii_vatican_council/documents/vat-ii_const_19651207_gaudium-et-spes_en.html.

Giffords Law Center to Prevent Gun Violence (n.d.). *Cover page*. Retrieved on 10/6/2021 from https://giffords.org/lawcenter/gun-laws/.

Giroux, H.A. (1988). *Teachers as intellectuals: Toward a critical pedagogy of learning*. South Hadley, MA: Bergin & Garvey Publishers, Inc.

Giroux, H.A. (2020). *On critical pedagogy* (2nd edition). London: Bloomsbury.

Glatz, C. (2021, Mar. 26). Pope says he, too, kneels on Myanmar streets, begging for end to violence. *The Catholic Leader*. Retrieved on 1/19/2022 from https://catholicleader.com.au/news/pope-says-he-too-kneels-on-myanmar-streets-begging-for-end-to-violence/.

Goizueta, R.S. (1995). *Caminemos con Jesus: Toward a Hispanic/Latino theology of accompaniment* (p. 209). Maryknoll, NY: Orbis Books.

Goodlad, J.I., Soder, R., & Sirotnik, K.A. (Eds.) (1990). *The moral dimensions of teaching*. San Francisco: Jossey-Bass Publishers.

Graf, N. (2018, Apr. 18). Pew Research Center (2018, April 18). A majority of U.S. teens fear a shooting could happen at their school, and most parents share their concern. Retrieved on 10/4/2021 from https://www.pewresearch.org/fact-tank/2018/04/18/a-majority-of-u-s-teens-fear-a-shooting-could-happen-at-their-school-and-most-parents-share-their-concern/?utm_source=Pew+Research+Center&utm_campaign=04bca95fdf-EMAIL_CAMPAIGN_2018_04_18&utm_medium=email&utm_term=0_3e953b9b70-04bca95fdf-400191633.

Gravissimum Educationis (1965, Oct. 28). Declaration on Christian education gravissimum educationis. Proclaimed by his holiness Pope Paul VI. *The Holy See*. Retrieved on 5/31/2021 from https://www.vatican.va/archive/hist_councils/ii_vatican_council/documents/vat-ii_decl_19651028_gravissimum-educationis_en.html.

Gremillion, J. (Ed.) (1976). *The gospel of peace and justice: Catholic social teaching since Pope John*. Maryknoll, NY: Orbis Books.

Griffin, M., & Block, J.W. (Eds.) (2013). *In the company of the poor: Conversations with Dr. Paul Farmer and Fr. Gustavo Gutiérrez*. Maryknoll, NY: Orbis Books.

Grim, D.W. (1994). Therapist spiritual and religious values in psychotherapy. *Counseling and Values, 38*, p. 154.

Grimes, M.L. (1996). Middle-class morality: Postures toward the poor. *National Forum, The Phi Kappa Journal, 76*(3), pp. 3–4.

Groome, T.H. (2019). *Faith for the heart: A "Catholic" spirituality*. Mahwah, NJ: Paulist Press.

Gun Violence Archive (n.d.). *Explainer*. Retrieved on 5/27/2022 from https://www.gunviolencearchive.org/.

Gun Violence Statistics (n.d.). Giffords law center to prevent gun violence. Retrieved on 10/04/2021 from https://giffords.org/lawcenter/gun-violence-statistics/#footnote_3_55.

Gutiérrez, G. (1973). *A theology of liberation, history, politics, and salvation* (Translated by Sister C. Inda, & J. Eagleson). New York, NY: Orbis Books.

Gutiérrez, G. (1984). *We drink from our own wells* (Translated by M. O'Connell). Maryknoll, NY: Orbis Books.

Gutiérrez, G. (1987). *On Job: God–talk and the suffering of the innocent* (Translated by M. O'Connell). Maryknoll, NY: Orbis Books.

Gutiérrez, G. (1990). *The truth shall make you free: Confrontations* (Translated by M. O'Connell). Maryknoll, NY: Orbis Books.

Gutiérrez, G. (1991). *The God of life*. Maryknoll, NY: Orbis Books

Gutiérrez, G. (1993). *Las Casas: In search of the poor of Jesus Christ* (Translated by R. Barr). Maryknoll, NY: Orbis Books.

Gutiérrez, G. (1996). Preferential option for the poor. *Conference at Perkins School of Theology at Southern Methodist University*.

Gutiérrez, G. (2003, Feb. 3). Remembering the Poor: An interview with Gustavo Gutierrez (with D. Hartnett) *America, 188*(3) (para. 10–11). Retrieved on 6/24/2021 from https://www.americamagazine.org/faith/2003/02/03/remembering-poor-interview-gustavo-gutierrez.

Gutiérrez, G. (2013). The option for the poor arises from faith in Christ. In P. Farmer, & G. Gutiérrez, *In the company of the poor: Conversations with Dr. Paul Farmer and Fr. Gustavo Gutiérrez* (Edited by M. Griffin, & J. W. Block) (pp. 147–59). Maryknoll, NY: Orbis Books.

Gutiérrez, G. (2015). Where will the poor sleep? In G. Gutiérrez, & G.L. Müller, *On the side of the poor: The theology of liberation* (Translated by R.A. Krieg, & J.B. Nickoloff) (pp. 83–133). Maryknoll, NY: Orbis Books.

Hackett, C., & McClendon, D. (2017, Apr. 5). Christians remain world's largest religious group, but they are declining in Europe. *Pew Research Center*. Retrieved on 2/26/2021 from https://www.pewresearch.org/fact-tank/2017/04/05/christians-remain-worlds-largest-religious-group-but-they-are-declining-in-europe/.

Harlan, C., & Loveluck, L. (2021, Mar. 5). Pope Francis lands in Baghdad, beginning the first-ever papal trip to Iraq. *Washington Post*. Retrieved on 3/13/2021 from https://www.washingtonpost.com/world/middle_east/pope-francis-iraq-2021/2021/03/05/097e2234-7aab-11eb-8c5e-32e47b42b51b_story.html.

Heath, E. (2021, Apr. 30). Italy has a gun culture but no mass shootings—here's why. *Reader's Digest*. Retrieved on 9/28/2021 from https://www.rd.com/article/italy-gun-culture/.

Helminiak, D. (1987). *Spiritual development.* Chicago, IL: Loyola University Press.

Hennelly, A.T. (Ed.) (1990). *Liberation theology: A documentary history.* New York: Orbis Books.

Hill, W.J. (1987). Theology. In J.A. Komonchak, M. Collins, D.A. Lane, *The new dictionary of theology*. Collegeville, MN: The Liturgical Press.

History.com Editors (n.d.). Second amendment. *A&E Television network*. Retrieved on 9/20/2021 from https://www.history.com/topics/united-states-constitution/2nd-amendment.

History.com Editors (2019, 2009). Industrial Revolution. *A&E Television Networks*. Retrieved on 11/24/2021 from https://www.history.com/topics/industrial-revolution/industrial-revolution.

Ignatius (n.d.). *Ignatius to the Smyrnaeans.* Eternal Word Television Network (EWTN). Retrieved on 12/22/2021 from https://www.ewtn.com/catholicism/library/ignatius-to-the-smyrnaeans-12519.

Inglis, W.B. (1959). Personalism, analysis, and education. *International Review of Education*, 5(4), pp. 383–99.

Jacobs, R.M. (1996). *The vocation of the Catholic educator.* The NCEA Catholic Educational Leadership Monograph Series. Washington, DC: National Catholic Educational Association.

Julian of Norwich (n.d.). *Revelations of divine love* (Translated by G. Warrack). Christian Classics Ethereal Library. Retrieved on 2/24/2022 from https://ccel.org/ccel/j/julian/revelations/cache/revelations.pdf.

King, M.L. Jr. (1967). *Where do we go from here: Chaos or community?* New York: Harper & Row Publishers.

Keating, T. (1997). *Open mind, open heart: The contemplative dimension of the gospel.* New York: Continuum.

Kerr, S. (2022, May 24). In K. Andrews, Warriors' Steve Kerr delivers impassioned plea for gun control after Texas school shooting: "We can't get numb to this" (para. 6). *ESPN*. Retrieved on 5/28/2022 from https://www.espn.com/nba/story/_/id/33979219/warriors-steve-kerr-delivers-impassioned-plea-gun-control-texas-school-shooting-get-numb-this.

Kirylo, J.D. (2011). *Paulo Freire: The man from Recife*. New York, NY: Peter Lang.

Kirylo, J. (2021). *The thoughtful teacher: Making connections with a diverse student population*. Lanham, MD: Rowman & Littlefield.

Kirylo, J.D., & Aldridge, J. (2019). *A turning point in teacher education: A time for resistance, reflection and change*. Lanham, MD: Rowman & Littlefield.

Kirylo, J.D., & Boyd, D. (2017). *Paulo Freire: His faith, spirituality, and theology*. Rotterdam, Netherlands: Sense.

Knudson, A.C. (1969). *The philosophy of personalism. A study in the metaphysics of religion*. New York-Cincinnati: Abingdon, 1927; reprinted, New York: Kraus Reprint.

Koch, J. (2009). *So you want to be a teacher?: Teaching and learning in the 21st century*. Boston, MA: Houghton Mifflin Company.

Kolander, C.A., & Chandler, C.K. (1990, Mar.). Spiritual health: A balance of all dimensions. Paper presented at the annual meeting of the AAHPERD National Convention, New Orleans, LA.

Komonchak, J.A., Collins, M., & Lane, D.A. (Eds.) (1987). *The new dictionary of theology*. A Michael Glazier Book. Collegeville, MN: The Liturgical Press.

Konyn, C. (2021, Aug. 24). What are carbon sinks? *Earth.Org*. Retrieved on 11/27/2021 from https://earth.org/carbon-sinks/.

Kreeft, P. (2017). *Catholics and Protestants: What can we learn from each other?* San Francisco: Ignatius Press.

Laity (n.d.). Encyclopedia.com. Retrieved on 3/14/2021 from https://www.encyclopedia.com/philosophy-and-religion/bible/bible-general/laity.

Lalli, T. (1999, Sep. 1). *Dom Helder Camara: Poet, mystic, missionary* (para 3). Retrieved on 6/12/2021 from http://www.jmm.org.au/articles/31316.htm.

Langan, H.E. (1935). *The philosophy of personalism and its educational applications*. Ph.D. diss. The Catholic University of America.

Lay Catholics in schools: Witnesses to faith (1982, Oct. 15). *The sacred congregation for Catholic education*. Retrieved on 3/21/2021 from https://www.vatican.va/roman_curia/congregations/ccatheduc/documents/rc_con_ccatheduc_doc_19821015_lay-catholics_en.html.

Lee, S. (2019, Jun. 7). How the "good guy with a gun" became a deadly American fantasy. *The Conversation*. Retrieved on 10/5/2021 from https://

theconversation.com/how-the-good-guy-with-a-gun-became-a-deadly-american-fantasy-117367.

Leean, C. (1988). Spiritual and psychosocial life cycle tapestry. *Religious Education, 83*(1), pp. 45–51.

Lernoux, P. (1980). *Cry of the people.* New York: Penguin Books.

Lewis, C.S. (1960). *The four loves.* San Diego: A Harvest Book, Harcourt Brace and Company.

Lewis, J. (2020). In J. Meacham *His truth is marching on: John Lewis and the power of hope.* New York: Random House.

Llort, Fernando (n.d.). Retrieved on 6/21/2022 from https://www.fernando-llort.com/biography.

Los textos de Medellín y el proceso de cambio en america latina primera edición (1977) (Translated by M. Hernandez-Lehmann). San Salvador Centroamerica: UCA/Editores.

Lovett, S.P. (2020, Mar. 24). Remembering St Oscar Romero: 40 years after his assassination. *Vatican News.* Retrieved on 6/13/2021 from https://www.vaticannews.va/en/church/news/2020-03/oscar-romero-forty-years-assassination-anniversary0.html.

Lu, M. (2013, Mar.). Aristotle on abortion and infanticide. *International Philosophical Quarterly, 53*(1), Issue 209, pp. 47–62.

Lumen, Gentium (1964, Nov. 21). *The Holy See.* Promulgated by His Holiness Pope Paul VI (Ch. 4, section 33). Retrieved on 3/15/2021 from http://www.vatican.va/archive/hist_councils/ii_vatican_council/documents/vat-ii_const_19641121_lumen-gentium_en.html.

MacMillan, A., & Turrentine, J. (2021, Apr. 7). Global warming 101. *Natural Resources Defense Council (NRDC).* Retrieved on 11/30/2021 from https://www.nrdc.org/stories/global-warming-101.

Martin, J. (2019, Jan. 10). Why I am pro-life. *America.* Retrieved on 11/11/2021 from https://www.americamagazine.org/2019/01/07/martin-why-i-am-pro-life.

MacCulloch, D. (2010). *Christianity: The first three thousand years.* New York: Viking.

Mcdonagh, E. (1987). Love. In J.A. Komonchak, M. Collins, D.A. Lane, *The new dictionary of theology* (pp. 602–16). Collegeville, MN: The Liturgical Press.

Maizland, L. (2021, Nov. 17). Global climate agreements: Successes and failures. *Council on Foreign Relations.* Retrieved on 12/2/2021 from https://www.cfr.org/backgrounder/paris-global-climate-change-agreements.

McElwee, J.J. (2021, Jan. 11). Pope Francis suggests people have moral obligation to take the coronavirus vaccine. *National Catholic Reporter.* Retrieved on 8/22/2021 from https://www.ncronline.org/news/vatican/ pope-francis-suggests-people-have-moral-obligation-take-coronavirus-vaccine.

McGovern, A.F. (1989). *Liberation theology and its critics: Toward an assessment.* Maryknoll, NY: Orbis Books.

McNeill, D.P., Morrison, D.A., & Nouwen, H. (1982). *Compassion: A reflection on the Christian life* (Drawings by J. Filartiga). New York: Doubleday.

Merton, T. (1961). *New seeds of contemplation.* New York: New Directions.

Merton, T. (1987). *Thoughts in solitude.* New York: Abbey of Our Lady of Gethsemani: Farrar, Straus, & Giroux Publishing.

Milani, L. (1957). *Esperienze pastorali* (Pastoral experiences). Firenze: Libreria Editrice Fiorentina.

Moore, K.A., Redd, Z., Burkhauser, M., Mbwana, K., & Collins, A. (2009, Apr.). Children in poverty: Trends, consequences, and policy options. *Child Trends Research Brief* (Publication #2009–11). Retrieved on 7/10/2021 from https://www.atlanticphilanthropies.org/wp-content/ uploads/2015/09/Child_Trends-2009_04_07_RB_ChildreninPoverty. pdf.

Moore, M.E.M. (2004). *Teaching as a sacramental act.* Cleveland, Ohio: The Pilgrim Press.

Morneau, R. (1983). *Spirituality and social justice* (Cassette Recording No. 7). Canfield, OH: Alba House Cassettes.

Mother Teresa Center (n.d.). *Biography.* Retrieved on 1/13/2022 from https:// www.motherteresa.org/biography.html.

Mother Teresa (1979). Mother Teresa acceptance speech. *The Nobel Prize.* Retrieved on 1/14/2022 from https://www.nobelprize.org/prizes/ peace/1979/teresa/acceptance-speech/.

Mother Teresa (1994, Sept. 9). Statement to Cairo conference on population. Retrieved on 5/7/2022 from https://www.ewtn.com/catholicism/library/ statement-to-cairo-conference-on-population-2700.

Mother Teresa (1996). *Mother Teresa: In my own words* (Compiled by Jose-Luis Gonzalez- Baldo). New York: Gramercy Books.

Mother Teresa (2015). In Statement of Fr. Brian Kolodiejchuk, MC, postulator of the cause of canonization of Blessed Mother Teresa. *Mother Teresa Center.* Retrieved on 1/14/2022 from https://www.motherteresa.org/08_ info/2015-Coversion.html.

Mounier, E. (1938). *A personalist manifesto* (Translated from the French by monks of St. John's Abbey). London: Longmans, Green and Co.

Mounier, E. (1952). *Personalism*. London, England: Routledge & Kegan Paul, LTD. (Translated by P. Mairet). *Le personnalisme* (First published in France, 1950).

Mounier, E. (1962). *Be not afraid: A denunciation of despair*. New York: Sheed and Ward.

Mounier, E. (1995, Mar.). Emmanuel Mounier and personalism. *Houston Catholic Worker, XV*(2). Retrieved on 04/16/2021 from https://cjd.org/1995/03/01/emmanuel-mounier-and-personalism/.

Muggeridge, M. (1980). *The end of Christendom*. Grand Rapids, MI: William B. Eerdmans Publishing Company.

NASA (n.d.). Scientific consensus: Earth's climate is warming. *Global Climate Change: Vital Signs of the Climate*. Retrieved on 11/ 30/2021 from https:// climate.nasa.gov/scientific-consensus/.

National Conference of Catholic Bishops (1986). *Economic justice for all: Pastoral letter on Catholic social teaching and the U.S. economy*. Washington, DC: United States Catholic Conference.

Neuman, W. (2015). Pope Francis lands in Ecuador to begin South America trip. New York Times. Retrieved on 10/6/2022 from http://www.nytimes.com/2015/07/06/world/americas/francis-hailed-as-pope-of-the-people-arrives-in-ecuador-on-3-nation-tour.html?_r=1.

New World Encyclopedia (2019, Jul. 29). Roman Catholic church. Retrieved 19:25, 2/20/2021 from https://www.newworldencyclopedia.org/p/index.php?title=Roman_Catholic_Church&oldid=1022655.

Nogales, A. (2018, Jan. 31). We live in a culture of violence. *Psychology Today*. Retrieved on 10/5/2021 from https://www.psychologytoday.com/us/blog/family-secrets/201801/we-live-in-culture-violence.

Nogrady, B (2021, Oct. 13). "I hope you die": How the COVID pandemic unleashed attacks on scientists. *Nature*. Retrieved on 5/10/2022 from https://www.nature.com/articles/d41586-021-02741-x.

Nostra, Aetate (1965, Oct. 28). Declaration on the relation of the church to non-Christian religions Nostra Aetate. Proclaimed by His Holiness Pope Paul VI (Part V). *The Holy See*. Retrieved on 3/7/2021 from https://www.vatican.va/archive/hist_councils/ii_vatican_council/documents/vat-ii_decl_19651028_nostra-aetate_en.html.

Nouwen, H.J.M. (1979). *Clowning in Rome: Reflection on solitude, celibacy, prayer, and contemplation*. New York: Image Books.

Nouwen, H.J.M. (1983). *Gracias: A Latin American journal.* Maryknoll, NY: Orbis Books.

Nouwen, H.J.M. (1984). Foreword. In G. Gutierrez, *We drink from our own wells: The spiritual journey of a people* (pp. xiii–xxi). New York: Orbis Books.

Nouwen, H. (2016). *The spiritual life: Eight essential titles.* New York: HarperOne.

NPR (2021, Aug. 18). In a message to Americans, Pope Francis says getting vaccinated is "an act of love." *National Public Radio.* Retrieved on 8/22/2021 from https://www.npr.org/sections/coronavirus-live-updates/2021/08/18/1028740057/in-a-message-to-americans-pope-francis-says-getting-vaccinated-is-an-act-of-love.

Nunez, C. (2019, Apr. 2). What are fossil fuels? *National Geographic.* Retrieved on 11/27/2021 from https://www.nationalgeographic.com/environment/article/fossil-fuels.

Nunez, E, A. (1985). *Liberation theology* (Translated by P. Sywulka). Chicago, IL: Moody Press.

O'Brien, D.J., & Shannon, T.S. (Eds.) (1977). *Renewing the earth: Catholic documents on peace, justice, and liberation.* New York, NY: Image Books.

O'Collins, G., & Farrugia, E.G. (1991). *A concise dictionary of theology.* New York: Paulist Press.

O'Grady, C. (2022, Mar. 24). In the line of fire. *Science.* Retrieved on 5/11/2022 from https://www.science.org/content/article/overwhelmed-hate-covid-19-scientists-face-avalanche-abuse-survey-shows.

O'Malley, J.W. (2009, Mar. 30). The complex history of indulgences. *America: The Jesuit Review.* Retrieved 1/30/2021 from https://www.americamagazine.org/issue/692/signs/complex-history-indulgences.

Ong, W. (1990, Apr. 7). "Yeast." Boston College (Office of University Mission and Ministry). Originally printed in *America*, and reprinted with Permission of American Press, Inc. Retrieved on 2/23/2021 from https://www.bc.edu/content/dam/files/offices/mission/pdf1/cu13.pdf.

Online Etymology Dictionary (n.d., a). *Catholic.* Retrieved on 2/21/2021 from https://www.etymonline.com/search?q=catholic.

Online Etymology Dictionary (n.d., b). *Ecumenical.* Retrieved on 3/6/2021 from https://www.etymonline.com/word/ecumenical?ref=etymonline_crossreference.

Overby, P. (2012, Dec. 21). NRA: "Only thing that stops a bad guy with a gun is a good guy with a gun." *NPR.* Retrieved on 10/04/2021 from https://

www.npr.org/2012/12/21/167824766/nra-only-thing-that-stops-a-bad-guy-with-a-gun-is-a-good-guy-with-a-gun.

Patriarch Bartholomew (2015). In Pope Francis, *Laudato si': On care for our common home*. Encyclical Letter. Huntington, IN: Our Sunday Visitor Publishing Division.

Percy, W. (n.d.). Famous author Walker Percy opposed abortion. Retrieved on 10/30/2021 from https://clinicquotes.com/famous-author-walker-piercy-opposed-abortion.

Perrigo, B. (2020, Oct. 23). The U.K. is facing a child hunger crisis. A sports star won't wait for the government to act. *Time*. Retrieved on 7/20/2021 from https://time.com/5903453/marcus-rashford-child-food-poverty/.

Pinar, W. (1994). *Autobiography, politics, and sexuality: Essays in curriculum theory, 1972–1992*. Dubuque, IA: Kendall/Hunt

Pinar, W., & Grumet, M.R. (1976). *Toward a poor curriculum*. Dubuque, IA: Kendall/Hunt

Pinar, W., Reynolds, W., Slattery, P., & Taubman, P. (1995). *Understanding curriculum*. New York: Peter Lang Publishing.

Poggioli, S. (2015, Nov. 1). Nostra Aetate' opened up Catholic, Jewish relations 50 years ago. *NPR*. Retrieved on 3/6/2021 from https://www.npr.org/2015/11/01/453448972/nostra-aetate-opened-up-catholic-jewish-relations-50-years-ago.

Poggioli, S. (2016, Oct. 28). The Pope commemorates the Reformation that split western Christianity. *NPR*. Retrieved on 3/10/2021 from https://www.npr.org/sections/parallels/2016/10/28/499587801/pope-francis-reaches-out-to-honor-the-man-who-splintered-christianity.

Pontifical Council for Justice and Peace (2004). *Compendium of the social doctrine of the church*. Washington, DC: United States Conference of Catholic Bishops.

Pope Benedict (2010). For the celebration of the world day of peace: If you want to cultivate peace, protect creation. *Libreria Editrice Vaticana*. Retrieved on 1/10/2022 from https://www.vatican.va/content/benedict-xvi/en/messages/peace/documents/hf_ben-xvi_mes_20091208_xliii-world-day-peace.html.

Pope Benedict VI (2011, Nov. 28). Address of his holiness Benedict XVI to students participating in a meeting promoted by the "sister nature" foundation. *Libreria Editrice Vaticana*. Retrieved on 12/2/2021 from https://www.vatican.va/content/benedict-xvi/en/speeches/2011/november/documents/hf_ben-xvi_spe_20111128_sorella-natura.html.

Pope Francis (2013, Jun. 12). General Audience (St. Peter's Square). *Libreria Editrice Vaticana*. Retrieved on 1/24/2022 from https://www. vatican.va/content/francesco/en/audiences/2013/documents/papa-francesco_20130612_udienza-generale.html.

Pope Francis (2013). Evangelii Gaudium (The Joy of the Gospel). *Libreria Editrice Vaticana*. Retrieved on 6/21/2022 from https://www.vatican.va/ content/francesco/en/apost_exhortations/documents/papa-francesco_ esortazione-ap_20131124_evangelii-gaudium.html.

Pope Francis (2015). *Laudato si': On care for our common home*. Encyclical Letter. Huntington, IN: Our Sunday Visitor Publishing Division.

Pope Francis (2020a). *The encyclical letter fratelli tutti: On fraternity and social friendship*. Mahwah, NJ: Paulist Press.

Pope Francis (2020b, Oct. 15). In R. Gomes Pope, Global Compact on Education bears in itself "a seed of hope." *Vatican News*. Retrieved on 4/2/2021 from https://www.vaticannews.va/en/pope/news/2020-10/pope-francis-global-compact-education-video-message-relaunch.html.

Pope Francis (2020c, Sept. 15). In P. Pullella, Pope urges respect for Paris climate accord, says "creation is groaning." *Reuters*. Retrieved on 12/2/2021 from https://www.reuters.com/article/climatechage-pope/ pope-urges-respect-for-paris-climate-accord-says-creation-is-groaning-idUSKBN25S4PV.

Pope Francis (2021, Mar. 26). In C. Glatz, Pope says he, too, kneels on Myanmar streets, begging for end to violence. *The Catholic Leader*. Retrieved on 1/19/2022 from https://catholicleader.com.au/news/pope-says-he-too-kneels-on-myanmar-streets-begging-for-end-to-violence/.

Pope John Paul II (1986, Apr. 13). Meeting with the Jewish community in the synagogue of the city of Rome. *Libreria Editrice Vaticana* (Part 3). Retrieved on 3/9/2021 from https://www.vatican.va/content/john-paul-ii/it/ speeches/1986/april/documents/hf_jp-ii_spe_19860413_sinagoga-roma.html.

Pope John Paul II (1987, Dec. 30). *Sollicitudo Rei Socialis* (The Social Concerns of the Church). Libreria Editrice Vaticana. 38. Retrieved on 7/21/2021 from https://www.vatican.va/content/john-paul-ii/en/ encyclicals/documents/hf_jp-ii_enc_30121987_sollicitudo-rei-socialis. html#-12.

Pope John Paul II (1995, Mar. 25). Evangelium vitae (The Gospel of life). *Libreria Editrice Vaticana*. Retrieved on 11/12/2021 from https://www. vatican.va/content/john-paul-ii/en/encyclicals/documents/hf_jp-ii_ enc_25031995_evangelium-vitae.html.

Pope John Paul II (2001, Jan. 17). General audience (God made man the steward of creation). *Libreria Editrice Vaticana*. Retrieved on 11/30/2021 from https://www.vatican.va/content/john-paul-ii/en/audiences/2001/documents/hf_jp-ii_aud_20010117.html.

Pope Leo XIII (1942). *On the condition of the working classes (Rerum Novarum)*. Boston: St. Paul Books & Media.

Pope Paul VI, & Patriarch Athenagoras I (1965, Dec. 7). Joint Catholic-Orthodox declaration of his holiness Pope Paul VI and the ecumenical Patriarch Athenagoras I. *Libreria Editrice Vaticana*. Retrieved on 2/26/2021 from http://www.vatican.va/content/paul-vi/en/speeches/1965/documents/hf_p-vi_spe_19651207_common-declaration.html.

Pope Paul VI (1967). *On the development of peoples (Populorum Progressio)*. Boston: St. Paul Editions.

Pope Paul VI (1970, May 17). In Educating to fraternal humanism. Building a "civilization of love": 50 years after populorum progression (para 29, note 35). Congregation for Catholic Education. *The Holy See* (2017, Apr. 16). Retrieved on 3/23/2021 from http://www.vatican.va/roman_curia/congregations/ccatheduc/documents/rc_con_ccatheduc_doc_20170416_educare-umanesimo-solidale_en.html#_ftnref35.

Pope Pius XI (1929, Dec. 31). Divini illius magistri. *Libreria Editrice Vaticana*. Retrieved on 4/2/2021 from http://www.vatican.va/content/pius-xi/en/encyclicals/documents/hf_p-xi_enc_31121929_divini-illius-magistri.html.

Praying Nature with St. Francis of Assisi (n.d.). Retrieved on 11/16/2021 from http://www.praying-nature.com/index.php.

Rafferty, J.P. (n.d.). The rise of the machines: Pros and cons of the industrial revolution. *Encyclopedia Britannica*. Retrieved on 11/27/2021 from https://www.britannica.com/story/the-rise-of-the-machines-pros-and-cons-of-the-industrial-revolution.

Ray, S. (2005). What does Catholic mean? *Catholic Answers*. Retrieved on 2/21/2021 from https://www.catholic.com/magazine/print-edition/what-does-catholic-mean.

Richert, S.P. (2019). What are the 4 cardinal virtues? *Learn Religions*. Retrieved on 5/14/2021 from https://www.learnreligions.com/the-cardinal-virtues-542142.

Roberts, P. (2000). *Education, literacy, and humanization: Exploring the work of Paulo Freire*. Westport, CT: Bergin & Garvey.

Roccasalvo, J.L. (2013, Oct. 9). Yeast in the dough. Catholic News Agency (CNA). Retrieved on 2/23/2021 from https://www.catholicnewsagency.com/column/yeast-in-the-dough-2699.

Rocha, F. (2009, Jan. 26). The red bishop. *Commonweal*. Retrieved on 6/12/2021 from https://www.commonwealmagazine.org/red-bishop.

Rohr, R. (1987a). *Beyond our cultural biases: Siding with the cosmic Christ*. Cincinnati: St. Anthony Messenger Tapes.

Rohr, R. (1987b). Silence and willing service: Delivery and mystery. Cassette 415. Series: *Letting Go: A Spirituality of Subtraction*. Cincinnati, OH: St. Anthony Messenger Press.

Rohr, R. (1999). *Everything belongs: The gift of contemplative prayer*. New York: The Crossroad Publishing Company.

Rohr, R. (2013). *Immortal diamond: The search for our true self*. San Francisco: Josey-Bass.

Rohr, R. (2019). *The universal Christ: How a forgotten reality can change everything we see, hope for, and believe*. New York: Convergent Books.

Rohr, R. (2020, Jul. 12). *Contemplation: A life's journey*. Center for Action and Contemplation. Retrieved on 2/26/2022 from https://cac.org/contemplation-a-lifes-journey-2020-07-12/.

Romero, O. (1978). In J.R. Brockman (Ed.) (1988), *The violence of love: The pastoral wisdom of Archbishop Oscar Romero* (Translated and compiled by James R. Brockman). New York: Harper & Row.

Romero, O. (1979). In J.R. Brockman (Ed.), *The violence of love: The pastoral wisdom of Archbishop Oscar Romero* (Translated and compiled by James R. Brockman). New York: Harper & Row.

Romero, O. (1984). In G. Gutiérrez, *We drink from our wells: The spiritual journey of a people*. Maryknoll, NY: Orbis Books.

Rose, M. (1995). *Possible lives: The promise of public education in America*. New York: Penguin Books.

Sacrament (n.d.). *Online etymology dictionary*. Retrieved on 1/26/2022 from https://www.etymonline.com/word/sacrament.

Sacred Congregation for the Doctrine of the Faith (1974, Jun. 28). *Declaration on procured abortion*. Retrieved on 10/25/2021 from https://www.vatican.va/roman_curia/congregations/cfaith/documents/rc_con_cfaith_doc_19741118_declaration-abortion_en.html.

Sahgal, N. (2017, Oct. 27). 500 years after the reformation, 5 facts about Protestants around the world. *Pew Research Center*. Retrieved on

2/26/2021 from https://www.pewresearch.org/fact-tank/2017/10/27/500-years-after-the-reformation-5-facts-about-protestants-around-the-world/.

Saint Francis (2015). In Pope Francis, Homily of His Holiness Pope Francis, Vatican Basilica. *Libreria Editrice Vaticana*. Retrieved on 1/14/2022 from https://www.vatican.va/content/francesco/en/homilies/2015/documents/papa-francesco_20150629_omelia-pallio.html.

San Martín, I. (2015, May 12). Liberation theology founder praises new "atmosphere" under Pope Francis. *Crux: Taking the Catholic Pulse* Retrieved on 6/3/2021 from https://cruxnow.com/church/2015/05/liberation-theology-founder-praises-new-atmosphere-under-pope-francis/.

Sanger, D.E., Lipton, E., Sullivan, E., & Crowley, M. (2020, Mar. 22). Before virus outbreak, a cascade of warnings went unheeded. *The New York Times*. Retrieved on 8/22/2021 from https://www.nytimes.com/2020/03/19/us/politics/trump-coronavirus-outbreak.html.

Sandel, M. (2020, Aug. 28). In C. Walsh Why some Americans refuse to social distance and wear masks. *The Harvard Gazette*. Retrieved on 8/23/2021 from https://news.harvard.edu/gazette/story/2020/08/sandel-explores-ethics-of-what-we-owe-each-other-in-a-pandemic/.

Saunders, W.P. (n.d.). What is the filioque clause? *Catholic Straight Answers*. Retrieved on 3/2/2021 from https://catholicstraightanswers.com/what-is-the-filioque-clause/.

Sawchenko, L.D. (2013). *The concept of person: The contribution of Gabriel Marcel and Emmanuel Mounier to the philosophy of Paul Ricoeur*. Master of Arts Thesis, Department of Religious Studies, Calgary, Alberta, Canada.

Schenker J.G. (2008). The beginning of human life: Status of embryo. Perspectives in Halakha (Jewish Religious Law). *Journal of Assisted Reproduction and Genetics*, 25(6), pp. 271–6. https://doi.org/10.1007/s10815-008-9221-6.

Schmelzer, E. (2019, Apr. 22). "I'll keep you safe": Teachers' anxiety over school shootings persists post-Columbine. *Governing: The future of states and localities*. Retrieved on 10/4/2021 from https://www.governing.com/archive/tns-teacher-anxiety-over-school-shootings.html.

Schubeck, T.L. (1993). *Liberation ethics: Sources, models, and norms*. Minneapolis, MN: Fortress Press.

Schuttloffel, M.J. (1999). *Character and the contemplative principal*. Washington, DC: National Catholic Educational Association

Schuttloffel, M.J. (2008). *Contemplative leadership: Creating a culture for continuous improvement.* Washington, DC: National Catholic Educational Association

Schuttloffel, M.J. (2019*). International explorations of contemplative leadership in Catholic education.* New York, NY: Routledge, Taylor & Francis Group.

Sensoy, Ö., & DiAngelo, R. (2017). *Is everyone really equal: An introduction to key concepts in social justice education* (2nd edition). New York: Teachers College Press.

Shusterman, N. (2018, Feb. 22). What the second amendment really meant to the founders. *The Washington Post.* Retrieved on 9/17/2021 from https://www.washingtonpost.com/news/made-by-history/wp/2018/02/22/what-the-second-amendment-really-meant-to-the-founders/.

Sigmund, P.E. (1988). The development of liberation theology: Continuity or change. In *The politics of Latin American liberation theology: The challenge to U.S. public policy* (Edited by R.L. Rubenstein, & J.K. Roth) (pp. 21–47). Washington, DC: The Washington Institute Press.

Silber, T.J. (1980, Fall). Abortion: A Jewish view. *Journal of Religion and Health, 19*(3), pp. 231–9. https://doi.org/10.1007/BF00990141.

Slavin, R.E. (2000). *Educational psychology: Theory and practice* (6th edition). Boston: Allyn and Bacon.

Slattery, P. (1995). *Curriculum development in the postmodern era.* New York: Garland Publishing.

Smith, C. (1991). *The emergence of liberation theology.* Chicago: The University of Chicago Press.

Stefon, M. (2012). *Christianity: History, belief, and practice.* New York, NY: Britannica Educational Publishing.

Tanner, N. (2011). *New short history of the Catholic church.* London: Bloomsbury.

Thawng, A.N. (2021, Dec. 8). In M. Bowling, Nun is honoured for holding her ground in the face of security forces. *The Catholic Leader.* Retrieved on 1/19/2022 from https://catholicleader.com.au/news/nun-is-honoured-for-holding-her-ground-in-the-face-of-security-forces/.

The Miami Herald Editorial Board (2022, May 27). In *The State* (Columbia, SC) Mass shootings: Don't pretend we can do nothing, p. 9A, para. 1–5, 8.

Unitatis Redintegratio (Decree on Ecumenism) (1964). *The Holy See.*
    Retrieved on 3/6/2021 from https://www.vatican.va/archive/hist_councils/
    ii_vatican_council/documents/vat-ii_decree_19641121_unitatis-
    redintegratio_en.html.

United States Conference of Catholic Bishops (2011). *Sharing Catholic social
    teaching: Challenges and directions.* Retrieved on 5/24/2021 from https://
    www.usccb.org/resources/sharing-catholic-social-teaching-challenges-
    and-directions.

United States Conference of Catholic Bishops (2020, Jan.). Backgrounder
    on Gun Violence: A mercy and peacebuilding approach to gun violence.
    Retrieved on 10/12/201 from https://www.usccb.org/resources/
    backgrounder-gun-violence.

Ut Unum Sint (On Commitment to Ecumenism) (1995, May 25). *Libreria
    Editrice Vaticana.* Retrieved on 3/8/2021 from http://www.vatican.va/
    content/john-paul-ii/en/encyclicals/documents/hf_jp-ii_enc_25051995_
    ut-unum-sint.html.

Van Doren, C. (1991). *A history of knowledge.* New York: Ballantine Books.

Vygotsky, L. (1978). *Mind in society: The development of higher psychological
    processes* (Edited by M. Cole, V. John-Steiner, S. Scribner, & E.
    Souberman). Cambridge, MA: Harvard University Press.

Wallis, J. (2005). *God's politics: Why the right gets it wrong and the left doesn't
    get it.* New York: HarperSanFrancisco.

Walter, J.J. (1987). Virtue. In J.A. Komonchak, M. Collins, D.A. Lane, *The new
    dictionary of theology* (pp. 1081–5). Collegeville, MN: The Liturgical Press.

Warren, M. (1988). Catechesis and spirituality. *Religious Education, 83*(1), pp.
    116–32.

Weidenkopf, S. (2018). *Timeless: A history of the Catholic church.* Huntington,
    IN: Our Sunday Visitor Publishing Division.

Whitehead, K.D. (1996, May/Jun.). How did the Catholic church get her
    name. *Our Sunday Visitor* (The Catholic Answer), Huntington, IN.
    Retrieved on 2/20/2021 from https://www.ewtn.com/catholicism/
    teachings/how-did-the-catholic-church-get-her-name-120.

Williams, T.D., & Bengtsson, J.O. (2016, Summer edition). Personalism. In
    The stanford encyclopedia of philosophy (Edited by E.N. Zalta). Retrieved
    on 4/15/2021 from http://plato.stanford.edu/archives/sum2016/entries/
    personalism.

World Central Kitchen (n.d.). Retrieved on 1/19/2022 from https://wck.org/
    en-us/story.

World Council of Churches (n.d.). Retrieved on 3/4/2021 from http://www.
oikoumene.org.

Yardley, J., & Neuman, W. (2015). In Bolivia, Pope Francis apologizes for
Church's "grave sins". (para 4). *New York Times*. Retrieved on 6/2/2021
from https://www.nytimes.com/2015/07/10/world/americas/pope-francis-
bolivia-catholic-church-apology.html?_r=0.

Zentner, M.H. (2015). The black death and its impact on the church and
popular religion. *Honors Theses 682*. Retrieved on 1/30/2021 from https://
egrove.olemiss.edu/hon_thesis/682.

Zwick, M., & Zwick, L. (2005). *The Catholic worker movement: Intellectual and
spiritual origins*. Reprinted p. 115, from *The Catholic Worker*, April, 1950.
New York/Mahwah, NJ: Paulist Press.

Index